BREAKTHROUGH WORKFORCE STRATEGY

Talent Insights and Proven Practices for a Competitive Difference

Breakthrough Workforce Strategy

Talent Insights and Proven Practices for a Competitive Difference

By Eric J. Seubert
Foreword by Thomas Casey
Epilogue by R.B. Stroud

Breakthrough Workforce Strategy
Talent Insights and Proven Practices for a Competitive Difference
All Rights Reserved.
v3.0

Edited by Amanda Tonkin

This publication is designed to provide accurate and authoritative information in regard to the subject matter covered. It is sold with the understanding that the publisher is not engaged in rendering legal, accounting or other professional services. If legal advice or other expert assistance is require, the services of a competent professional person should be sought.

Outskirts Press, Inc.
http://www.outskirtspress.com

ISBN: 978-0-578-07957-8

Library of Congress Control Number: 2011923180

Outskirts Press and the "OP" logo are trademarks belonging to Outskirts Press, Inc.

PRINTED IN THE UNITED STATES OF AMERICA

ALSO BY ERIC SEUBERT

Talent Readiness: *The Future is Now*
with Thomas Casey and Timothy Donahue

ACKNOWLEDGEMENTS

Mom and Dad.
Thank you for nurturing my curiosity and drive.

Virginia.
Thank you for loving me. Thank you for giving me strength
to pursue my ambition. Thank you for being my friend.

My Children.
Thank you for showing interest in this book. You are a bless-
ing in my life.

God.
Thank you for the inspiration and wisdom to write this
book.

CONTENTS

FOREWORD

Just when you thought you could relax as the recession dissipates Eric Seubert comes along and confronts us with an even more sobering reality. **How will we plan and execute our growth strategies when demographics are shifting, engagement is declining, and those with critical skills are disappearing into retirement?**

How do we plan our workforce needs in the U.S. when the fastest growing segment of talent contains those over the age of 55? How far can France push elevation of the retirement age to 62 if the trade-off for a solvent system is infrastructure paralysis? How will Japan cope when its essentially homogeneous workforce will need to include more than 20% non-ethnic citizens to subsidize its social benefits? Moreover, to whom rests the responsibility to create the Workforce Plan?

There was a book published by Dr. Noel Tichy entitled *Control Your Destiny Or Somebody Else Will!* This title is prophetic for those responsible for safeguarding the talent pipeline, development and retention at the Enterprise level. Presently the lack of clarity regarding the implications of the above and concomitant lack of robust planning to cope portend calamity!

The lack of progressive or even evasive answers to the question "what is our workforce plan" are now becoming indefensible for those chartered to — you guessed it — have a plan!

In his book, *Breakthrough Workforce Strategy*, Eric is in many ways throwing us all a life preserver when we need it the most! He frames for us the emerging trends, implications for a lack of responsiveness, and when we feel anti depressants are the only solution, an outstanding framework for developing a Workforce Plan

The book *Breakthrough Workforce Strategy* is *recommended* reading for all who want to understand the implications of these shifting dynamics and an *essential* read for those of us who are being held accountable for enterprise planning.

- Tom

Thomas Casey is the Managing Principal of Discussion Partner Collaborate, a global Executive Advisory firm focused on Human Capital Strategy.

INTRODUCTION

If you do not understand what a workforce strategy is, you are not alone. I have been architecting strategies for years and my own mother still does not understand it.

So, let me explain it this way. Does your organization want to: *hire top-performing candidates, reduce voluntary departures, mitigate retirement turnover* or *build a talent supply chain?* *Breakthrough Workforce Strategy* can help you achieve that, and more, by showing you insights and proven practices of a critical position workforce strategy. The framework, tools and templates illustrated here will help your organization put the *right workers* in the *right jobs* at the *right time* so the business organization can achieve outcomes like sales growth, on-time shipments, engaged customers or workplace safety.

If that interests you, then come with me. I will show you how it is done.

Until we speak…all the best,

- Eric

Part I

Setting the Table

CHAPTER 1

This Time, Conventional Wisdom is Wrong

Conventional Wisdom

Conventional wisdom believes labor in America is abundant. This seems logical since in 2010, alone, we have had a pool of unemployed workers hovering around 14 million or 10% of the workforce. The trouble is, this time, conventional wisdom is false and many executives are risking not having "the right workers, with the right skills, in the right jobs, at the right time."

Talent Strategy Advisors recently completed a three-and-a-half-year study of labor market data, from January 2007 through June 2010, to determine the truth behind the abundant labor claim. Figure 1-1 shows the number of unemployed workers has been building for some time. In fact, during 2010, the U.S. economy has averaged 14.1 million unemployed workers during each of the first six months.

Figure 1-1

U.S. Unemployed Workforce: Jan 2007 - Jun 2010

U.S. Bureau of Labor and Statistics Data

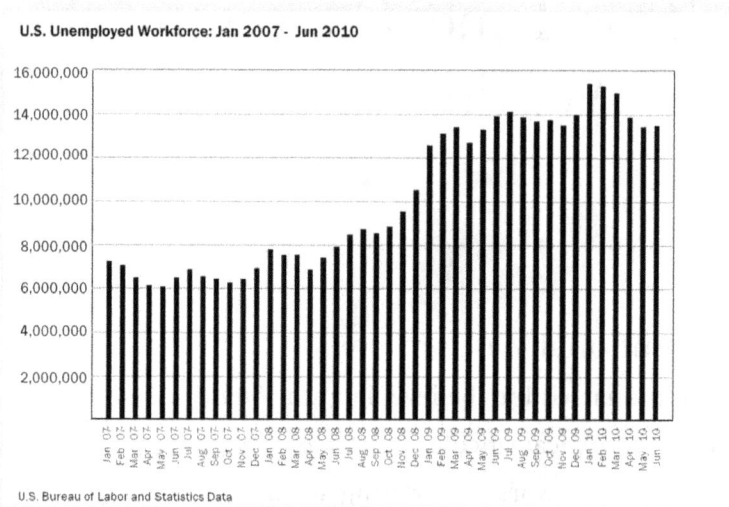

The Truth About the Workforce

With so many unemployed, it is reasonable to believe the economy has an ample supply of workers. Yet, when data one level below the macro-economy is examined, a different story unfolds. For example, in June 2010, 85% of the unemployed workers were from 25% of the economy's occupations

[Figure 1-2]. Included in this group are jobs like cashier, construction supervisor, and production worker. This means while the recession has touched all sectors, its impact has been contained to a few occupations. The truth is, the majority of occupations in the U.S. are not significantly contributing to the unemployment rate and this is in fact a trend that has been occurring since at least January 2007.

Figure 1-2

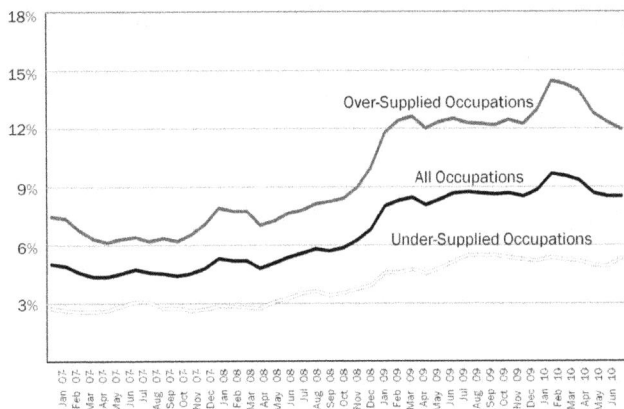

U.S. Unemployed Rate: Jan 2007 - Jun 2010

U.S. Bureau of Labor and Statistics Data

If only a few U.S. occupations are significantly contributing to the unemployment rate, how are the remaining occupations being affected by the recession?

To answer this question, we searched for occupations with an unemployment rate at or below 6%, and found that a startling 46% of the U.S. economy's occupations meet this criteria. Included in these occupations are jobs like actuary, bus driver, truck mechanic, register nurse and sales engineer.

The large number of jobs is significant because at 4% unemployment, a workforce is considered fully employed; a state where everyone wanting to work, has a job. With almost one of every two occupations near full employment, it seems the U.S. workforce is signaling that some occupations may have too few workers. Figure 1-3 confirms the 237 occupations, labeled Group A, and the 274 occupations, labeled Group B, have maintained lower and higher levels of unemployment, respectively, since January 2007, the beginning of this study. Supporting Figure 1-3 are Figures 1-4 and 1-5 which depict examples of jobs in both Group A and B.

So, while layoffs from the recession have increased the unemployment rate for Group B, the slow-down in hiring has also triggered the unemployment rate rise in Group A. The recession hasn't solved the talent shortage for Group A occupations – it is only delaying it.

Figure 1-3

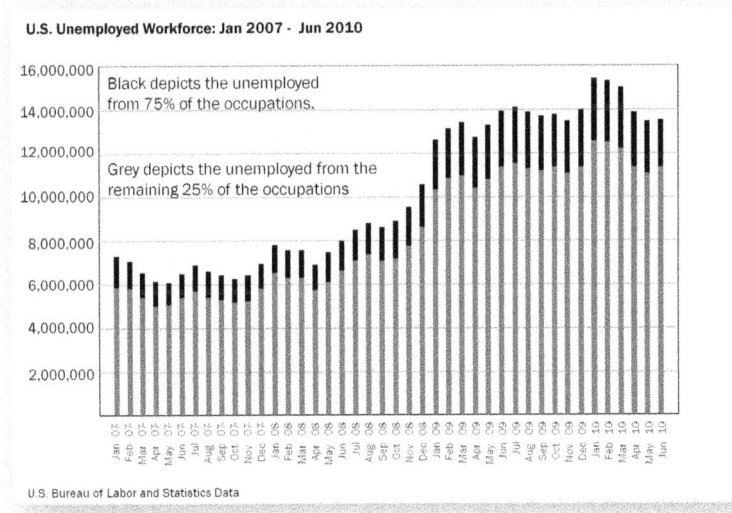

U.S. Unemployed Workforce: Jan 2007 - Jun 2010

Black depicts the unemployed from 75% of the occupations.

Grey depicts the unemployed from the remaining 25% of the occupations

U.S. Bureau of Labor and Statistics Data

Figure 1-4

Group A Example Occupations

- Accountants
- Actuaries
- Air traffic controllers
- Aircraft mechanics
- Aircraft pilots and flight engineers
- Bus drivers
- Bus and truck mechanics
- Database administrators
- Engineers: aerospace, biomedical chemical, civil, environmental, geological, software, mining, nuclear and petroleum

- Engineering managers and supervisors
- Maintenance supervisors
- Medical scientists
- Occupational therapists
- Physician assistants
- Power plant operators
- Production supervisors
- Register nurses
- Retail sales supervisors
- Sales engineers
- Utility meter readers

Figure 1-5

Group B Example Occupations

- Advertising sales agents
- Assemblers and fabricators
- Cashiers
- Child care workers
- Computer programmers
- Construction laborers
- Construction supervisors
- Cooks
- Electricians
- Home health aids
- Hotel desk clerks
- Loan officers
- Machinists
- Millwrights
- Order clerks
- Plumbers & pipefitters
- Production workers
- Security guards
- Sheet metal workers
- Retail salesperson
- Textile workers
- Waiters & waitresses
- Waiters & waitresses supervisors

TWO GROWING TRENDS

Now, when we further examine Group A occupations, we see two concerning trends. These occupations have a higher percentage of workers, age 55 and older [Figure 1-6] …

Figure 1-6

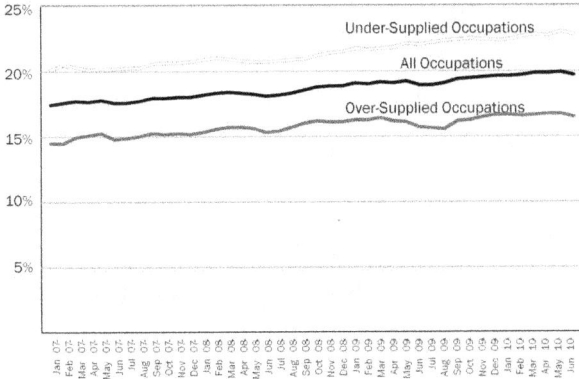

U.S. Workers Age 55 and Older Percentage: Jan 2007 - Jun 2010

Under-Supplied Occupations

All Occupations

Over-Supplied Occupations

U.S. Bureau of Labor and Statistics Data

and a lower percentage of younger, Generation Y workers, born between 1980 and 2000 [Figure 1-7].

Figure 1-7

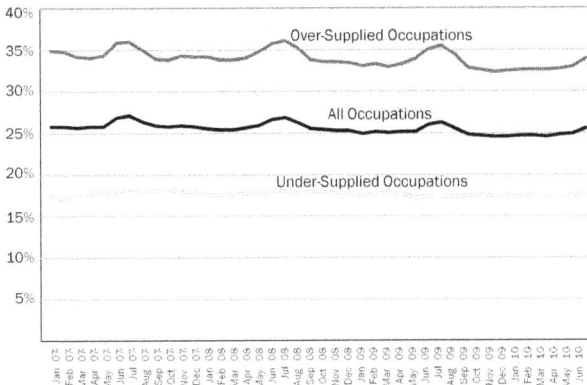

U.S. Gen Y Workers Percentage: Jan 2007 - Jun 2010

Over-Supplied Occupations

All Occupations

Under-Supplied Occupations

U.S. Bureau of Labor and Statistics Data

Our conclusion is while the U.S. economy has a large number of unemployed, these workers are from a small segment of occupations. In fact, 46% of the U.S. occupations have 6% or less unemployment. Since almost one of every two occupations is near full employment it would be prudent for executives to take precautionary attraction and retention actions, regardless of whether their organization's workforce is growing. Turnover in Group A occupations will likely result in extended search periods for replacement workers.

CHAPTER 2

The Making of a Workforce Strategy

Detecting a Trend

By 2006, it was obvious that companies were going to face a new challenge. As Ken Dychtwald, Tamara Erickson and Robert Morison proved in their groundbreaking book, *Workforce Crisis*, America was, and is, experiencing an aging population, driven by three demographic realities: a baby boomer bubble, longevity boom and birth dearth. The combined result is an unprecedented shift in population age and workforce composition.

In the spring of 2006, two colleagues, Tom Casey and Tim Donahue, and I began to believe that executives would value a framework and toolkit for managing this changing workforce. By summer, Tom, Tim and I had collaborated on a business process that integrates multiple human capital initiatives into a global talent supply chain for meeting current and future enterprise goals. We attractively titled this business process a "workforce strategy."

Since then, several features of the framework have undergone enhancements, yet its core functions have stood the test of time and remained virtually unchanged, namely, its usefulness helping executives:

- Create organization buy-in for a workforce strategy

- Forecast attraction, retention, engagement and performance risks

- Evaluate core human resources processes for opportunities to not only strengthen their effectiveness, but also better enable the strategic intents of the workforce strategy

- Secure qualified workers for the organization's most important roles

- Design a roadmap to transition from strategy design to tactical implementation

A Workforce Strategy Framework

The framework, which we use on consulting and advisory projects, guides us in evaluating internal and external workforce risks using demographic data, performance assessments, talent metrics and supply and demand models. The distinguishing feature of the framework is its workforce intelligence capability — a unique capacity to generate powerful workforce insights drawn from a workforce forecasting tool. These insights are crucial to producing a compelling workforce strategy for our consulting and advisory clients.

Figure 2-1 depicts our approach to building a workforce strategy. The PLAN stage begins the workforce strategy with two processes that establish the management procedures and scope of the initiative. The COMMIT stage is next and includes a process that justifies the workforce strategy initiative. The DIAGNOSE stage determines risks and opportunities to an organization's most important roles and lastly, the RECOMMEND stage finishes with a process that architects the human capital recommendations and their implementation project plans. Together, these four stages and their processes produce the relevant components of a viable workforce strategy for resolving attraction, retention, engagement and performance challenges.

Figure 2-1

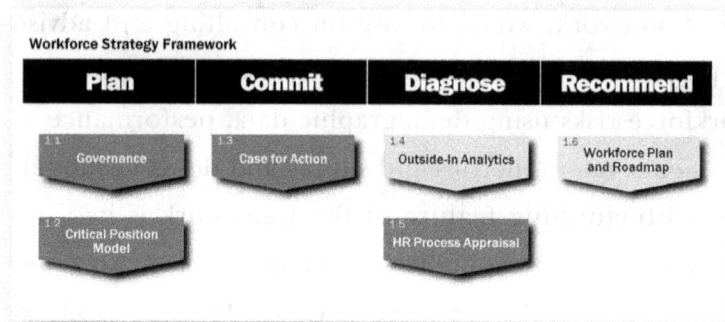

1.1 Workforce Strategy Governance

Workforce Strategy Governance is the primary set of activities for planning and controlling a workforce strategy initiative. This process coordinates development of four key work products that:

- Produce the vision and intents of the workforce strategy

- Establish accountability for key business outcomes

- Resolve potential and sometimes contentious issues associated with a workforce strategy

- Identify responsibility or ownership for key decisions in the development and implementation of a workforce strategy

1.2 Critical Position Model

The Critical Position Model is a prioritized list of the organization's most important roles; jobs that are mission critical and highly business impacting. This process includes activities for identifying the critical positions, relative to a specific set of criteria and prioritizing them, relative to a set of business outcomes and intents. The output is the initial subjects of the workforce strategy.

1.3 Case for Action

The Case for Action is an important work product that uncovers and organizes grounded evidence for a why a workforce strategy is needed. The process requires a diverse set of skills; *analytics*, which is used to sort through volumes of external labor market and internal workforce data to uncover issues and risks, and *communications*, which is used to frame a coherent "story" for an executive-level audience.

1.4 Outside-In Analytics

Outside-In Analytics includes two processes for determining the likelihood, severity and impact of human capital issues and risks to a critical position workforce. The detail, number-crunching work performed here provides the findings and conclusions that ultimately shape the recommendations of the workforce strategy. The issue and risk identification process begins with an activity that examines "external" labor market followed by a second activity that assesses "internal" workforce data.

1.5 Human Resources Process Appraisal

The Human Resources Process Appraisal is simply a performance improvement assessment to identify policy, procedure, organizational and technology opportunities within the HR operating model. So, while this process does not contribute directly to a critical position workforce strategy, its work produce does create a more effective HR infrastructure for launching a critical position workforce strategy.

1.6 Workforce Plan and Roadmap

The final process in the framework generates the Workforce Plan and Roadmap. The Workforce Plan is the set of recommendations to combat attraction, retention, performance and engagement issues and risks, and ensure an organization has the right workforce in the right critical position job, at the right time. The Roadmap is the implementation strategy and work plan for transitioning from the current state to the future.

These are the six steps of the workforce strategy framework. While our executive workshops explore this framework in more detail, for now, this high-level scan of "How" we build workforce strategies for our consulting and advisory clients will suffice. However, there is more.

Over the years, we have meticulously developed a compelling viewpoint regarding workforce strategies. This viewpoint has been honed into seven distinct insights, depicted in Figure 2-2. Seven practices which we use to separate our clients' strategy from the competition. Seven practices that enable our clients' to take a threat faced by every company and exploit it for their gain. Seven practices that along with the framework, create a Breakthrough Workforce Strategy.

Figure 2-2

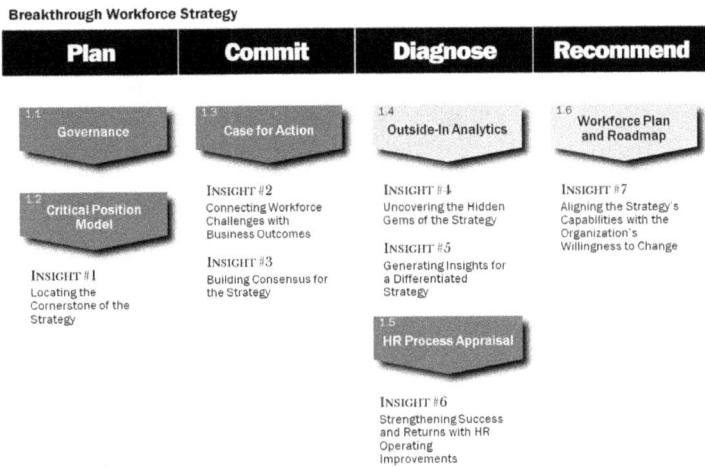

Part II

A Seven Course Banquet

CHAPTER 3

Locating the Cornerstone of the Strategy

How We Define a Problem Determines How We Solve It

Take for example a high school student who has always academically underperformed in school — maybe even demonstrates a bad attitude about learning. Some educators would look at this situation and instinctively think the child does not care and then write them off, but what other educators have come to realize is startling. Some of these students actually have undiagnosed learning disabilities which make it very difficult to learn using traditional classroom teaching methods. Overtime, some of these students have become discouraged, maybe even depressed or cynical.

So, while two students might share a common symptom, how the problem is defined will ultimately determine whether the solution is focused on student motivation or alternative teaching methods.

Identifying Which Workforce is Meant for the Workforce Strategy

The same concept applies to a workforce strategy. How we define the problem a workforce strategy is constituted to address determines how we solve it. A workforce strategy is not focused on application technologies, marketing plans or manufacturing processes. A workforce strategy is focused on resolving threats and risks to an organization's workforce — its human capital. Yet, depending on how a workforce is defined, an organization can have numerous workforces. There is the enterprise workforce, a workforce for each business unit and a workforce for each department. So, if a workforce strategy is to focus on a workforce, which one is it?

The answer to that question came to me while reading *Structure in Fives: Designing Effective Organizations* by Henry Mintzberg, an international author and expert in business and management. Mintzberg helped me see that a business is nothing more than workers divided into *orchestrated tasks,* called *jobs.* It doesn't matter whether the organization is a multi-billion dollar conglomerate, a small business or a twelve year old with a lawn cutting service. The concept that workers are organized by job applies. So, in terms of the question, "which workforce is the focus of a workforce strategy?" the answer appears to be the job.

Determining Which Jobs are Meant for the Workforce Strategy

Now, it is not enough to simply focus a workforce strategy on an organization's jobs. Some organizations can have upwards of 1,000 jobs! We have to have a method for prioritizing the positions so the jobs which are more influential to operations have their symptoms diagnosed and resolved before less-influential jobs.

When we think about the challenge of prioritizing jobs from a business point of view, the criteria most likely to produce an optimal sequence is the job's *contribution to the business' core activities.* We refer to jobs fitting this description as "critical positions."

So, while many business challenges are surrounded by lots and lots of data, only a few are actually relevant. In our case, what is most relevant and effective is to:

INSIGHT #1

*Focus the workforce strategy
on a critical position workforce*

So, how does an organization go about selecting its critical positions? We have found that most business executives have a good idea of which jobs are critical, but to give grounding to their instincts, we have a two test activity for determining if a position is critical or not.

Figure 3-1

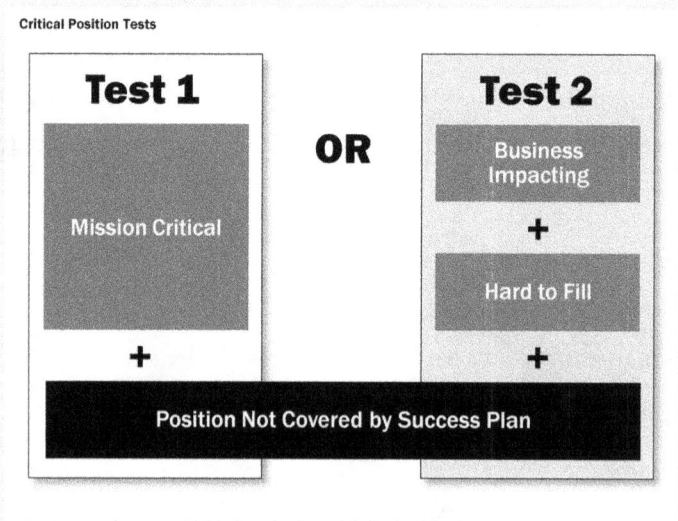

Critical Position Tests

Test 1	OR	Test 2
Mission Critical		Business Impacting
+		+
		Hard to Fill
		+
Position Not Covered by Success Plan		

In Figure 3-1, the first test for a critical position is whether or not it is "mission critical." This refers to a job whose workers must meet a licensing requirement, like airline pilots, ship engineers and nuclear power plant shift supervisors. Any job meeting test one is automatically considered a critical position. For those not meeting test one, we have a second test that evaluates a job for its "business impact" and "hard-to-fill" characteristics. A job is, by nature, business impacting if it significantly contributes to the organization's strategic business outcomes, such as, revenue, profits, customer experience, productivity or safety. For a job to be considered hard to fill, it must take, on average, two to two-and-one-half times longer to fill than the organization's average time-to-fill metric. Jobs which we frequently see satisfying test two include technical sales supervisor, plant general manager and many engineering roles, like nuclear, petroleum and mining.

Lastly, regardless of the test, for any job to be considered a critical position it also must be one that is not currently included in the organization's succession plan. This final criteria acknowledges that most organizations have already developed some sort of back-fill planning for their executive positions, as part of their succession planning effort. Therefore, this last criteria forces organizations to evaluate those jobs that might not be as "top-of-mind" as an executive-level job, but are, nonetheless, even more critical to the daily operations of the organization.

Six Characteristics of a Critical Position

Now, although we have a good foundation in the criteria for a critical position, there is still a little more. The criteria helps us determine if a position is critical, but it does not tell us everything. With that, let us explore six characteristics of a critical position.

1. Critical position priority changes as the business scenario changes.

Critical positions are prioritized to give focus to the organization regarding which positions are most important at a point in time. This prioritization is a function of the current business scenario. Change the business scenario and the prioritization of critical positions will change.

For example, at the beginning of the global economic recession, most companies were pursuing a scenario of "cost reduction." Then, as the economy began to show signs of a recovery, the business scenario changed, once again, to one focused on "revenue growth." The critical positions key to a cost reduction scenario are dramatically different than those for a revenue growth scenario. So, while the pool of critical positions infrequently changes, the prioritization of those critical positions do change with the business scenario.

2. Critical position unemployment rates are almost always lower than the national average.

Because critical positions are fundamental to an organization's strategy, workers in those occupations are almost always last to be let-go during a corporate downsizing. As a result, the unemployment rate for critical position occupations almost always lags the national unemployment average. For example, while the national unemployment average in September 2009 was 10.2%, several critical position occupations had averages far lower. For example, healthcare critical positions had an unemployment average of just 2.2% and sales critical positions were 5.4%.

Recognizing that the unemployed supply of critical potions workers almost always lags national averages will help executives make adjustments to attraction and retention strategies to reflect the tight critical position labor market.

3. Staffing a critical position takes at least twice as long as the average position.

Because of the supply and demand characteristics of critical position workforces, staffing a critical position job requires at least twice as much time as an organization's "typical" job. So, if the organization's "time to fill" measure is 94 days, meaning it takes 94 days from the time a position is posted to the time someone shows up to work on their first day, we can expect that staffing a critical position job in this organization will take at least 188 days or nearly six months.

4. Critical position supply lags demand during growth periods.

The constant demand and lower unemployment supply for critical-position workers translates into a shallow critical position labor pool. Therefore, when executives need to expand their workforces, particularly during growth periods, they quickly realize that the immediate supply of workers is insufficient, resulting in attraction breakdowns.

5. When supply lags demand, demand is strongest for critical positions requiring extensive experience and capabilities.

The steady demand and lower unemployment supply for critical- position workers translates into a shallow critical position labor pool. It's been observed that the pool is shallowest for those critical position workforces where the experience requirements are high or the key capabilities take years to develop. Examples of these critical positions include: energy trader, mining engineer, IT network architect or high-voltage utility lineman.

6. **The customer facing critical position workforce increases in strategic importance as the product or service nears commoditization.**

Customer facing critical positions are always vital to an organization. However, as the product or service they support loses their differentiating characteristics, it becomes critical the organization focuses on the customer experience as a means of differentiation. Since customer facing critical positions, like sales executives or customer support representatives, spend a considerable amount of time with customers, it is crucial that these critical positions create a positive experience – one that distinguishes the organization from its competitors.

A Validation Technique

After we have our list of critical positions, we like to run a quick validation to ensure the positions we have identified are truly business impacting to the organization. The tool we most frequently use for this is the Critical Position Alignment Model. Its intent is to demonstrate the alignment between a critical position and its business outcomes.

Figure 3-2

Critical Positions Alignment Model

Business Strategy			
25% top line growth across all three business units			
Business Outcomes			
Critical Positions	New Revenue Production	New Customer Prospecting	New Customer Satisfaction
Call Center Agent	◑	◑	●
Maintenance Engineer	○	○	◑
New Product Engineer	◑	○	◑
Plant Manager	○	○	◑
Production Shift Supervisor	○	○	◑
Sales Manager	●	●	◑

KEY: Low ○ ◔ Medium ◑ ◕ High ●

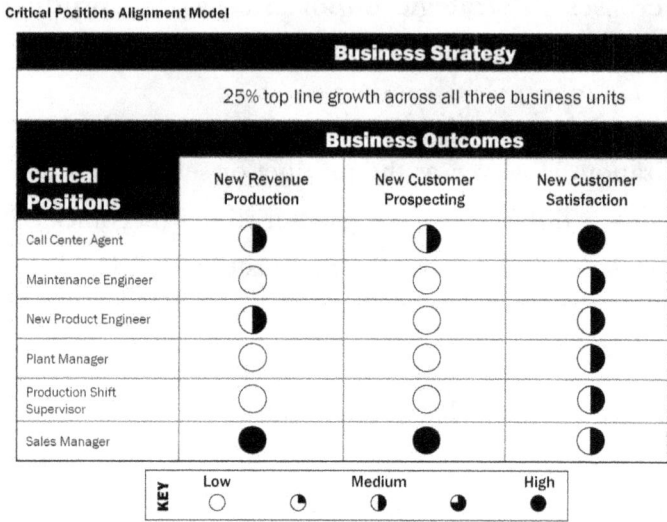

The Critical Position Alignment Model, Figure 3-2, consists of a:

- *Business Strategy* – A description of the organization's current strategic plan. Here it is expressed in terms of the current plan's goal.

- *Business Outcomes* – A description of the three-to-five things that have to occur in order for the business strategy to be achieved. Think strategic, here. If the organization does not achieve this list of outcomes, then the strategy's success is in jeopardy.

- *Critical Position Assessment* – Some type of relative assessment, whether using Harvey Balls or a numeric score, say from one to five with five being high, of the critical position's impact or contribution to each business outcome.

This model can be produced from interviews or a facilitated workshop with business stakeholders. Building this model with stakeholders really helps to create consensus that the organization is focusing on the right jobs for its workforce strategy.

We have yet to work with a company that has the luxury of making sub-optimal investments. An organization's workforce strategy is an investment. Firstly, it is an investment in people's time and eventually, an investment in interventions to address a critical position's issues and risks. To help executives allocate their human capital investments to assets with the best possible enterprise-wide impact or return potential, we encourage a workforce strategy focused on critical positions. The critical positions which run through the workforce strategy framework, first, are those that have a significant impact to the organization's business outcomes. Whether you use the Critical Position Alignment Model or not, it is still a prudent step to validate your critical positions relative to their ability to produce some type of business impact.

CHAPTER 4

Connecting Workforce Challenges With Business Outcomes

Any executive who has struggled to staff a critical position with qualified workers probably understands the connections between the workforce and the organization's business objectives. Why? Critical positions are the handful of jobs which have a direct and significant impact on business performance. A vacancy or under-qualified worker in a critical position means an organization has a chink in its armor. Now, the chink may never be exposed. Sometimes, arrows are directed at other parts of the armor, giving executives time to "repair" the gap, but if left unattended, it's likely the chink will eventually affect organizational operations and business results.

Because of the tight coupling between a critical position and business outcomes, a human resources issue, like challenges to attraction and retention is now considered a business issue. Yes, it is human capital related, but the potential risk to business performance elevates the status of this potential business challenge. Because of this, a workforce strategy is considered an integral part of modern business strategy. To bring this concept forth for the organization, workforce strategists should:

INSIGHT #2

*Socialize the business benefits
of the workforce strategy*

For many workforce strategists new to the position, this insight is as much for them as it is for the organization. This insight is really best accomplished in two steps and includes demonstrating WHY and HOW a workforce strategy has business impact and taking accountability for specific business outcomes.

Step 1: Discover WHY a Workforce Strategy is Business Impacting

It is important to be very clear in your mind why a workforce strategy is business impacting. This is particularly pertinent when you first introduce this concept to the organization, so let us walk though some previous findings.

Chapter 3 demonstrated for us the linkage between a workforce strategy and its business outcomes. In that chapter, we established the logic that:

- A workforce strategy is focused on a job's workforce – the workers associated with a job in the organization.

- The initial jobs included in the workforce strategy are called critical positions.

- Critical positions have a strong linkage to business outcomes because they are either mission critical or business impacting.

- The linkage between a critical position and the organization's business strategy and outcomes can be depicted in the Critical Position Alignment Model, Figure 3-2.

These four points and the supporting content explain WHY a workforce strategy is business impacting.

Step 2: Demonstrate HOW a Workforce Strategy is Business Impacting

The previous step established the general linkage between business outcomes and the workforce strategy. Step 2 helps the workforce strategist discover the linkages for a specific critical position.

In Hi-Tech organizations, technical sales is a critical position with a direct impact on the organization's business performance. The typical sales executive usually has an engineering or technical undergraduate or graduate degree, industry knowledge and several years of relevant product or service experience. In many sectors, good sales executives, not just high-performing ones, are difficult to attract and retain. As a result, many organizations are plagued by high turnover, long times to staff and unmet sales goals. With this example, here is how a workforce strategist can demonstrate the business impact of a critical position workforce strategy.

Begin by listing the symptoms of the position. Often, this is a summary of the human capital issues and risks plaguing the job. In this example, they are:

- Higher Turnover

- Lengthy Times to Staff

- Unmet Sales Goals

This list represents the things we need to fix which can

usually be ascertained by speaking with the Human Resources manager for the sales team, a sales supervisor or two and even the Head of Sales. At this moment, we do not know what is causing them, but we can agree that change needs to occur. So, the intended outcome from a technical sales executive workforce strategy must be:

- Reduced Turnover

- Faster Time to Staff

- Met or Exceeded Sales Goals

Next, if these workforce strategy outcomes are produced, determine which business targets would be impacted. This information can be obtained from someone in the sales organization, like a sales supervisor or the Head of Sales.

In the example we have, posing this question to sales executives would likely generate a list consisting of improvements in:

- Sales

- Profits

- Customer Experience

Now, let us return to our workforce strategy outcomes one more time and determine how these outcomes can be measured. Understanding this linkage is important to monitoring success and can be determined by anyone familiar with human resources or talent measures, like the workforce strategist or human resources manager. In the example, some likely measures for the three outcomes are:

- Reduced Turnover

    o Probationary Period Turnover

    o Involuntary Turnover

    o Voluntary Turnover

- Faster Time to Staff

    o Time to Staff

    o 1st Candidate Acceptance Rate

- Met or Exceeded Sales Goals

    o Time to Proficiency

    o Annual Review Scores

    o Position Standards Met or Exceeded

Now, the purpose of Step 2 is not to collect the information. Instead, it is to demonstrate or communicate it to stakeholders. A tool which Talent Strategy Advisors uses to do just this is called the *Business Value Relationship Diagram*, Figure 4-1.

Figure 4-1

Business Value Relationship Diagram

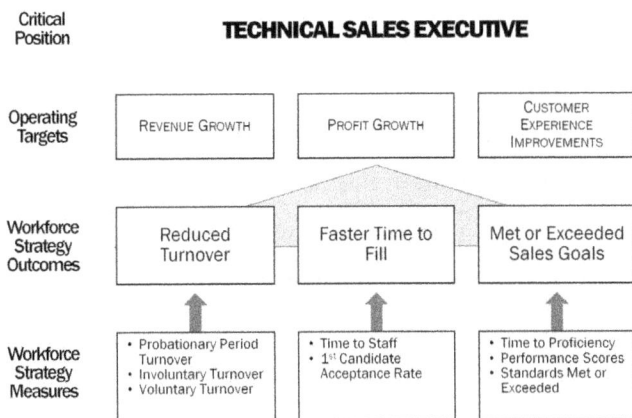

Critical Position	**TECHNICAL SALES EXECUTIVE**		
Operating Targets	REVENUE GROWTH	PROFIT GROWTH	CUSTOMER EXPERIENCE IMPROVEMENTS
Workforce Strategy Outcomes	Reduced Turnover	Faster Time to Fill	Met or Exceeded Sales Goals
Workforce Strategy Measures	• Probationary Period Turnover • Involuntary Turnover • Voluntary Turnover	• Time to Staff • 1st Candidate Acceptance Rate	• Time to Proficiency • Performance Scores • Standards Met or Exceeded

This tool is powerful because it visually demonstrates the connections making the workforce strategy business impacting. The diagram depicts a one-to-one relationship between the workforce strategy's outcomes and measures and a one-to-many relationship between the outcomes and the operating targets. What we really like about this tool is that it facilitates a conversation, whether using a single business executive or a group of stakeholders, regarding the business impact a workforce strategy can produce. We designed the chart that begins a conversation in the middle of the diagram with the workforce strategy outcomes. For example, after introducing the scope of the workforce strategy, in this case, a technical sales executive, we would discuss the symptoms that have been observed and how they are the focus of the solution. Next, we would explain that resolving the symptoms have a direct impact on key operating targets such as revenues, profits and customer experience. We usually share an example that reinforces the concept of having the right person, in the right job, at the right time, will contribute to our targets. Lastly, we say that we will be able to monitor our progress with the workforce strategy using, in this case, eight important measures. So, start in the middle with the outcomes. Link these to the targets and close with the measures.

Our experience shows that for a workforce strategy to succeed, it must be accepted by the organization as a business-impacting initiative. Organizations that insist their workforce strategy is simply a Human Resources project will likely under-deliver both human capital and business results. The Business Value Relationship Diagram is a tool the workforce strategist can use to demonstrate the strategy's power for producing business outcomes, like an organization's operating targets.

CHAPTER 5

Building Consensus for the Strategy

For most organizations, the phrase "workforce strategy" was not even in the corporate vernacular five years ago. It was not until around 2006 when demographic experts began speaking about baby boomer retirements that workforce supply risks became a relevant concern. Then 2008 ushers in a global recession and some executives proclaim that the risk has been resolve. In fact, all the economic downturn did for this risk was to slow hiring. It certainly did not resolve the demographic challenges underlying the risk. The need for a workforce strategy now is just as great as it was in the mid 2000.

The Need for Organizational Acceptance

I have found that those who have "doubts" about the need for a workforce strategy span a scale ranging from "still questioning" to "absolute disagreement." Unfortunately, for me, I discovered this finding the hard way. Our first couple of workforce strategy project allocated very little time and resources building consensus. Instead, we quickly moved right into the diagnostics stage. Then, within four to six weeks, word would leak to the organization of potential changes the workforce strategy might recommend. Not just process related changes, but the painful type ... cultural changes. This is when the "doubters" began to surface and objections began to fly like arrows at a burlap target. While I have a strong track-record for handling even the toughest claims against a workforce strategy, having to address a full-blown "appeals process" in the middle of a strategy project is a momentum-killing event. I estimate that in the projects where we put the strategy on hold in order to address concerns and achieve consensus, the net impact was a 1.5 to 2 times increase in the strategy's schedule and costs. We have seen that failing to adequately address the need for change not only creates confusion and negative perceptions about a workforce strategy, but it also adds to its timeline and total cost.

The most effective tactic for addressing internal organizational acceptance risks associated with a workforce strategy is to:

INSIGHT #3

Answer, early in the journey, the WHY, HOW and WHAT of the workforce strategy

The duration of a workforce strategy varies from business to business and is a function of many variables. So, when trying to schedule when to address the organization's questions, it's not possible to prescribe a specific week in the project schedule. Instead, what we coach others is to address the questions before 30% of the strategy project's time has elapsed and that the total time we are referring to is that consumed by the activities depicted in Figure 2-1. So, for a 12-week strategy project that includes Plan, Commit, Diagnose and Recommend activities, we would prepare to answer by the fourth week the organization's initial questions.

Now, what needs to be addressed in the beginning? In our experience, really only three questions:

1. WHY do we need a workforce strategy?

2. HOW are we building our workforce strategy?

3. WHAT will we get from the effort?

Question 1: WHY do we need a workforce strategy?

Try addressing this question by discussing the *Likelihood, Potential Severity* and *Possible Impact* the following situations could have on your organization: Cover those on the list that are relevant to your situation.

1. Explain that your industry's workforce is aging and that is increasing the risks of retirement turnover. Discuss how this could affect your organization's knowledge and expertise and its impact on the customer.

2. Discuss that the attitudes and beliefs of Generation Y entering the workforce are different than Boomers and Gen X and how this is increasing:

    a. Attraction risks

    b. Turnover risks

    c. Employee engagement

3. Show how over time, "where" the organization sourced its workers has dramatically changed and how staying current with these trends is crucial to recruiting the organization's future workforce.

4. Demonstrate how some occupations, even during the recession, had a low supply of workers and how this is

increasing vacancy (the amount of time to fill a job) and performance risks (lower workforce performance because under-qualified candidates are hired)

5. State that while the immediate case for a workforce strategy is largely based on industry trends, the project will examine our organization's workforce data to uncover our specific risks.

The hardest part about addressing these points is not getting wrapped up in the details. I like to say that the information at this point should be a mile wide and an inch deep. What I mean by this is that we want to be thorough in analyzing industry workforce data for risks, but we do not need to explain them to the nth degree of detail. Doing so creates the potential of getting lost in a sea of data and answering a never-ending set of "tell me more" questions from the organization.

Question 2: HOW are we Building Our Workforce Strategy?

This question is really about the techniques you will use to construct the workforce strategy. For some organizations, the question can be answered by having a conversation around the activities depicted in Figure 2-1's four stage framework.

For other organizations, a discussion on the following bullet points is enough to address HOW.

- Establish a governance protocol for planning and controlling the initiative

- Identify the organization's most important jobs, called critical positions and prioritize based on their impact to the current business operating measures

- Determine by critical position its workforce risks and issues stemming from internal and external attraction, retention, engagement and performance challenges.

- Identify other Human Resources process improvements which would contribute directly to our critical position workforce strategies.

- Generate targeted recommendations and work plans for the organization to review.

Question 3: WHAT will we Get from the Effort?

This question is not necessarily a discussion of sample workforce strategy recommendations. Instead, it is an opportunity to demonstrate the business impact that a workforce strategy can have on the organization's current operating measures, which was created while building the

Business Value Relationship Diagram, Figure 4-1. Simply discuss with the organization the connections between the workforce strategy as a set of recommendations for addressing a critical position's attraction, retention, engagement, performance risks and issues, and the *Likelihood, Potential Severity* and *Possible Impact* these critical position risks and issues can have on the organization's business outcomes.

In most organizations, the concept of a workforce strategy is relatively new. Its recent emergence means that most organizations have yet to understand, let alone, experience and appreciate the value of this initiative. A workforce strategy is similar to any other business project in that it introduces to the organization to some level of change. Creating the list of an organization's most pressing questions regarding a workforce strategy was intentionally created so workforce strategists could better inform the organization of the initiative's purpose and in result is frequently consensus for a workforce strategy and an easing of the organization into inevitable change opportunities.

CHAPTER 6

Uncovering the Hidden Gems of the Strategy

A demographic is simply a characteristic used to group people, like age, generation, culture or gender. In a workforce strategy we analyze demographics for insights into why specific events are occurring, like challenges with attraction, retention, engagement and performance.

Why Demographic Knowledge is Valuable

See, workers in certain demographic groups have something in common — something more than just the characteristic used to group them. We have found that certain demographic groups share similar beliefs and these beliefs trigger common and often, predictable behaviors. These similar or shared beliefs and predictable behaviors contribute valuable insights into why a demographic group produced a specific situation, like a steady increase in resignations. Now, sure, it is true that not EVERYONE within a demographic group share similar beliefs and behaviors, yet, understanding significant demographic segments of your workforce can help better pinpoint the cause of problems.

See, it is very possible that voluntary turnover may have different causes in two demographic segments of your workforce. Segments like Generation Y workers and Boomers or Hispanic culture workers and Caucasian-Americans. Understanding the different root causes will help you design not only a more effective solution, but a more efficient one. If you only remember one point from this chapter, I hope it is this. Workforces are not homogenous. The challenges you observe may fit nicely into prefabricated categories but the cause of those challenges can vary greatly. The days of a one-size-fits-all solution are over.

Now, the importance of demographics does not apply only to the internal workforce. The key to designing a strategy that successfully attracts, retains and engages workers is an understanding of the demographics making up the external labor market for each critical position. So, awareness of the segments and their contributions to the symptoms, as well as the segments making up a critical position's labor market, often turn out to be the hidden gems of a work-force strategy.

The most common method of analyzing a critical position workforce for its demographics is spreadsheet applications and their calculation, graphing tools and pivot table features. With an application, like Microsoft Excel, a workforce strategist can manipulate large volumes of workforce data, sort and filter worksheets for findings and conclusions and graphically view the analysis using bar charts, histograms and distributions.

Because demographics contribute such powerful insights, workforce strategies should:

INSIGHT #4

Analyze workforce demographics using a trio of characteristics to generate greater clarity into a critical position's issues and risks

As we mentioned above, there are many characteristics which can be used to describe a group, but not all are equally powerful. Figure 6-1 depicts the characteristics which we assess most frequently:

Figure 6-1

Workforce Characteristics Model

Demographic

Age
Gender
Generation
Education
Mobility
Occupation
Culture

Region
Density
Growth Pattern

Family Life-Cycle
Motives
Risk Tolerance
Attitudes

Geographic

Psychographic

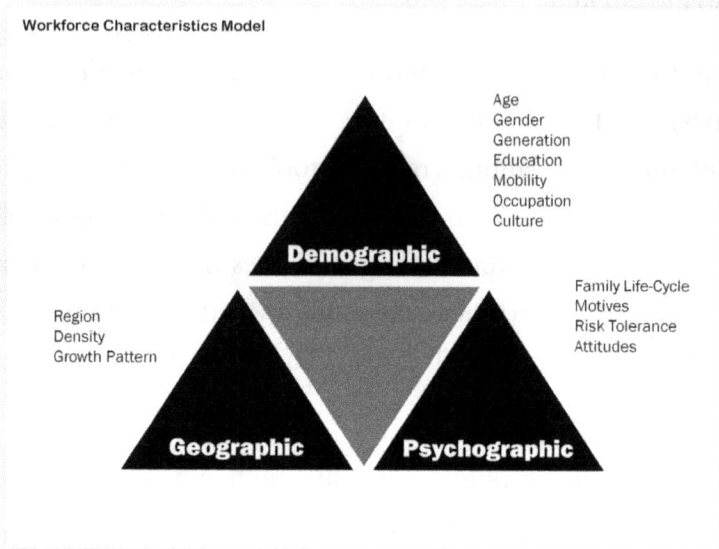

- *Personal:* The distinguishing characteristics of a worker.

- *Geographic:* The location a worker occupies.

- *Psychographic:* The Interests, Activities and Opinions of a worker (sometimes referred to as IAO).

Next, these demographics are relevant at different points in the Workforce Strategy Methodology. Assessing data by demographics is first performed in the COMMIT Stage when developing the Case for Action. It is then used again in the

DIAGNOSE Stage when determining external and internal workforce challenges. Lastly, it is used in the RECOMMEND Stage to design an efficient and effective workforce plan.

An Example of Demographic Analysis

To illustrate how demographics are used for analyzing workforce data, let us look at an example.

Most Americans have little awareness of the importance freight railroads play in our daily lives. Railroads transport 40% of American's freight, goods like coal, automobiles, foods, chemicals and lumber. Of all modes of transportation, trains carry the most freight, even transporting more than trucks by 50%. Railroads are efficient, environmentally friendly and safe and while they lack flexibility in routes, their benefits ensure a continued place in America's economy.

One occupation that is key to the railroad industry is the locomotive engineer. This job operates the cargo carrying trains, moving controls, monitoring conditions and making adjustments for things like grade and condition of the rail, the number of cars and the ratio of empty cars to loaded cars. A locomotive engineer must be federally licensed, making this position, not only business impacting, but also mission critical. Without a licensed engineer, a locomotive remains idle.

The steps we used to examine the demographics of the loco-motive engineer, or any occupation, began with determining the number of workers in the occupation.

Step 1- First Level Workforce Analytics

Data from the Bureau of Labor and Statistics reports that in June 2010, 49, 565 workers were employed in the occupation and 0% unemployment [Figure 6-2]. Therefore, our first findings from the analysis are:

> *Finding #1: The locomotive engineer occupation, in June 2010, has no slack supply.*

Figure 6-2

	Employed	Unemployed	Total
Locomotive Engineer	49,565	0	49,565

U.S. Bureau of Labor and Statistics Data

Step 2 – Second Level Workforce Analytics

Next, we conducted what we commonly refer to as Level 2 analysis by examining four different demographic segments of the locomotive engineer workforce: gender, generation, age and education. The findings from the Level 2 analysis [Figure 6-3] include:

Finding #2: The occupation employs 12% women, well-below the U.S. female workforce participation rate of 47%, yet above the rail industry rate of 5%.

Finding #3: The occupation has a Boomer to Gen Y ratio of 11, meaning that for every Gen Y worker, there are 11 Boomers. This is significantly higher, meaning we have fewer Gen Y workers, than the U.S. Boomer to Gen Y ration of 1.6 and the industry ratio of 5.0.

Finding #4: The occupation has 32% of its workforce age 55 or older, higher than the U.S. workforce of 20% and the industry of 24%.

Finding #5: 62% of the occupation has either college experience, without a degree (28%), an associate's degree (26%) or a bachelor's degree (8%) compared to 61% for the U.S. workforce and 55% for the industry.

Figure 6-3

GENDER	Male	Female	Total
Locomotive Engineer	43,526 88%	6,039 12%	49,565
U.S. Workforce	82,078,107 53%	71,764,515 47%	153,842,622
Railroad Industry	268,841 95%	15,462 5%	284,303

GENERATION	Gen Y	Gen X	Boomer	Traditionalist	Total
Locomotive Engineer	3,149 6%	14,002 28%	32,414 65%	- 0%	49,565
U.S. Workforce	38,723,406 25%	49,399,664 32%	57,970,746 38%	7,748,806 5%	153,842,622
Railroad Industry	30,974 11%	92,231 32%	153,534 54%	7,564 3%	284,303

EDUCATION	Did not graduate H.S.	H.S. degree, no college	Some college, did not graduate	Associates degree	Bachelors degree or higher	Total
Locomotive Engineer	2,091 4%	16,835 34%	13,878 28%	12,831 26%	3,930 8%	49,565
U.S. Workforce	15,384,262 10%	44,614,360 29%	29,230,098 19%	15,384,262 10%	49,229,639 32%	153,842,622
Railroad Industry	16,973 6%	110,327 39%	78,502 28%	33,947 12%	44,555 16%	284,303

AGE	55+
Locomotive Engineer	15,837 32%
U.S. Workforce	29,942,696 19%
Railroad Industry	67,776 24%

U.S. Bureau of Labor and Statistics Data

Step 3 – Third Level Workforce Analytics

Our Level Two analysis is followed by Level Three and it is at this point, where we believe we begin to uncover our hidden demographic gems. Level Three is not necessarily a new set of demographic categories. Instead, we combine two or more previously examined demographic groups to see if we can uncover a possible competitive advantage. Here is what we mean: In Level Two, we examined both generation and gender. Now, in Level Three, we examine the gender mix within each generation [Figure 6-4]. We also want to examine the generation mix within each education category [Figure 6-5]. After doing each, we discovered:

Finding #6: 0% of the occupations workforce is Gen Y – Females while the U.S. percentage is 11%, nearly equally to the Gen Y – Male participation rate of 13%. The industry Gen Y – Female participation rate is 1%.

Finding #7: 12% of the occupation's workforce is Gen X and Boomer Females compared to U.S. and industry percentages of 33% and 3%.

Finding #8: Only 6% of the occupation's workforce is Gen Y – Males while the U.S. percentage is 13%, and the industry Gen Y participation rate is 10%.

Finding #8: All 6% of the occupation's workforce that is Gen Y have at least attended college where only 58% of the

U.S. Gen Y workforce and 76% of the industry have some college credits.

Figure 6-4

EDUCATION - GENERATION	Gen Y	Gen X	Boomer	Trad	Total
Locomotive Engineer					
Did not graduate H.S.	-	2,091	-	-	2,091
H.S. degree no college	-	4,740	12,095	-	16,835
Some college, did not graduate	1,237	1,749	10,892	-	13,878
Associates degree	1,895	5,576	5,360	-	12,831
Bachelors degree or higher	-	-	3,930	-	3,930
					49,565
Did not graduate H.S.	0%	4%	0%	0%	
H.S. degree no college	0%	10%	24%	0%	
Some college, did not graduate	2%	4%	22%	0%	
Associates degree	4%	11%	11%	0%	
Bachelors degree or higher	0%	0%	8%	0%	
U.S. Workforce					
Did not graduate H.S.	4,496,932	5,076,577	5,031,261	779,492	15,384,262
H.S. degree no college	10,922,741	13,801,978	17,386,831	2,502,811	44,614,360
Some college, did not graduate	10,160,253	7,965,203	9,967,915	1,136,728	29,230,098
Associates degree	3,050,378	5,240,778	6,500,099	593,008	15,384,262
Bachelors degree or higher	8,447,854	18,033,929	19,900,918	2,846,938	49,229,639
					153,842,622
Did not graduate H.S.	3%	3%	3%	1%	
H.S. degree no college	7%	9%	11%	2%	
Some college, did not graduate	7%	5%	6%	1%	
Associates degree	2%	3%	4%	0%	
Bachelors degree or higher	5%	12%	13%	2%	
Railroad Industry					
Did not graduate H.S.	3,001	3,514	10,459	-	16,973
H.S. degree no college	4,168	41,456	56,827	7,876	110,327
Some college, did not graduate	12,590	22,812	43,100	-	78,502
Associates degree	2,219	15,697	16,031	-	33,947
Bachelors degree or higher	8,652	8,803	27,099	-	44,555
					284,303
Did not graduate H.S.	1%	1%	4%	0%	
H.S. degree no college	1%	15%	20%	3%	
Some college, did not graduate	4%	8%	15%	0%	
Associates degree	1%	6%	6%	0%	
Bachelors degree or higher	3%	3%	10%	0%	

U.S. Bureau of Labor and Statistics Data

Figure 6-5

GENERATION - GENDER	Gen Y	Gen X	Boomer	Traditionalist	Total
Locomotive Engineer					
Male	3,149	12,627	27,750	-	43,526
Female	-	1,375.00	4,664.00	-	6,039
					49,565
Male	6%	25%	56%	0%	
Female	0%	3%	9%	0%	
U.S. Workforce					
Male	20,550,417	26,907,735	30,348,260	4,271,695	82,078,107
Female	18,172,989	22,491,929	27,622,486	3,477,111	71,764,515
					153,842,622
Male	13%	17%	20%	3%	
Female	12%	15%	18%	2%	
Railroad Industry					
Male	27834	89622	147066	4319	268,841
Female	3140	2609	6469	3244	15,462
					284,303
Male	10%	32%	52%	2%	
Female	1%	1%	2%	1%	

U.S. Bureau of Labor and Statistics Data

Now, when it comes to resolving attraction and retention challenges, there are some real gems contained in these findings. We see six conclusions that are shaping potential recommendations.

The occupation:

> *Conclusion #1: Is under-supplied*

> *Conclusion #2: Has attraction risks because of its full-employment level.*

> *Conclusion #3: Has supply-gap risks because it does not have Gen Y workers to backfill retirements and routine turnover.*

Conclusion #4: Has retirement risks because of its high number of aging workers.

Conclusion #5: Has sourcing opportunities for mid-career female candidates.

Conclusion #6: Has sourcing opportunities at community colleges and some universities for Gen Y candidates, both male and female.

While many of the conclusions require further analysis before they can be shaped into a recommendation, at this point, it is apparent how examining a workforce by its different demographic groups can contribute to a workforce strategy with recommendations that have a competitive difference.

CHAPTER 7

Generating Insights for a Differentiated Strategy

We can measure things like time, distance, and volume which we do frequently to record statistics meaningful to an organization. Yet, when it comes to labor markets, executives do not have a meter, a gauge, or even a stick to determine the market's supply of qualified workers for their organization.

As early as five years ago, most organizations did not need to monitor workforce supply. Human Resources either advertised for jobs or contacted external recruiters and "presto" candidates appeared. Ok, for some jobs, it might not have been that easy, but most agree that attracting workers was not a top five business concern. The need to monitor workforce supply is about to change and we predict some organizations will use this capability to build a competitive advantage.

Why The Workforce Shortage is Not Going Away

Many can explain that the cause of the workforce shortage is demographic changes created by an aging population. But, it is more than just an aging population and understanding the complete problem is critical to accepting that this challenge is not going away.

Our aging population is a result of three inter-related phenomenon. Because of advances in healthcare, more people are living longer and fewer children are dying at a younger age. That is reason one and two. The third reason for the aging population is women are having fewer babies.

For generations, the world has experienced a growing population. From 1750 to 1950, the world's population grew from one billion to three billion people. Then, from 1950 to 2000, it doubled from three billion to six billion. Yet, in the midst of this growth, life-styles began to change.

In the 1800's experts believe the fertility rate, the average number of children born to a woman in her life, was around 6.0 to 8.0 in Europe and America. Fast-forward to today and the fertility rate is about 1.6 to 1.8. While the dramatic decline is eye-catching, there is another significant point about these numbers. To sustain a population experts have calculated the fertility rate at 2.1. Anything above 2.1 and the population will grow. Anything below and the population will decline. Because of our lower fertility rate, America's population will eventually decline and it's possible that this may occur as early as 2030.

So, while American's population trend projects growth for the next ten to twenty years because people are living longer, this growth will slow and eventually turn negative as a generation passes and the implications of a lower fertility rate takes effect.

If you think the workforce shortage introduced in Chapter One will resolve itself, think again. This phenomenon is here for at least as long as our careers.

A Measurement Tool To Refocus Attention on the Workforce Challenge

Very often, what we measure becomes the focus of our attention. If a measure indicates something is problem, most will fix it. Therefore, to help determine which critical positions will likely be affected by a worker shortage, it is recommended that organizations:

INSIGHT #5

Utilize workforce intelligence capabilities to identify critical positions with supply threats

Workforce intelligence is an emerging capability that forecasts critical position workforce supply and demand. Many of our early adopting clients are using this capability to improve business decisions and establish an advantage in their marketplace. The forecast is not intended to be precise and pin-point an exact number of workers for the supply and demand figures. Instead, its purpose is to depict supply and demand issues and trends for a critical position which executives can use to draw insights about a workforce and make better informed business decisions.

The forecast is fundamentally a stock and flow model for a specific workforce over a period of time. The model begins with a projection of the workforce demand and subtracts from it a projection of the supply, which is often the sum of several supply pool estimates. Common components of the workforce intelligence model include the following:

Demand Components

- *Sector Demand* – The workers employers require for their business plan. In most situations, we do not project demand by demand types, which is different than how supply is projected.

Supply Components

The supply pools listed here are potential components for the model. Not every pool is part of every model. Use only those pools that have a relevant and significant impact on the projection.

- *Employed* – The qualified workers employed in the occupation.

- *Unemployed* – The qualified workers unemployed, but seeking employment.

- *Other Qualified Workers* – Workers in similar occupations OR who are reentering the workforce after some time off who could be quickly re-trained and deployed for the occupation.

- *Graduates* – Workers entering the labor market from a trade school, community college or university.

- *Retirees Leaving the Workforce* – Workers exiting the occupation's labor market due to retirement.

- *Retirees Re-Entering the Workforce* – Workers who previously retired and have opted to reenter the occupation's labor market.

Given the potential insights available from such a model, executives should consider prioritizing which critical positions require workforce intelligence capabilities, first. The following offers an example of how this capability can be applied.

Expansion of the global economy and adoption of technologies that enable electronic package tracking and time-specific deliveries is fueling long-term growth prospects for the transportation industry. Unfortunately, long hours, weekend employment, labor-intensive jobs and out-dated work environments have dissuaded many younger workers from career opportunities in the industry. One critical position in the industry is the Class A Short-Haul Truck Driver. Workers for this position have a U.S. commercial driver's license permitting them to tractor-trailer trucks. This role is very different than long haul or overnight drivers. The short haul driver departs from a home base and usually makes several deliveries, within a single trip, unloading cargo at each stop before returning to their base at the end of the day. Often, short haul drivers have a regular route or delivery schedule. This position's business impactful nature within the transportation industry makes it an ideal candidate for a workforce intelligence model, which we have depicted in Figure 7-1.

Figure 7-1

Current Year Plus 5 Supply Gap Model Short-Haul Class A Truck Driver Critical Position

	2010	2011	2012	2013	2014	2015
DEMAND						
Sector Demand	1,493,924	1,553,681	1,615,828	1,680,461	1,747,680	1,817,587
TOTAL DEMAND	1,493,924	1,553,681	1,615,828	1,680,461	1,747,680	1,817,587
SUPPLY						
Employed	1,493,924	1,553,681	1,615,828	1,680,461	1,712,726	1,746,281
Unemployed	233,811	188,994	142,383	77,750	34,954	36,352
Other Qualfied Workers	47,291	47,707	48,127	48,550	48,978	49,409
Retirees Re-Entering Workforce	12,391	14,582	16,813	18,915	20,891	23,439
Retirees Leaving Workforce	(123,913)	(145,815)	(168,132)	(189,148)	(208,906)	(234,392)
TOTAL SUPPLY	1,663,504	1,659,148	1,655,020	1,636,528	1,608,642	1,621,089
Supply Gap	169,580	105,467	39,192	(43,933)	(139,038)	(196,498)
Supply Gap Percentage	10%	6%	2%	(3%)	(9%)	(12%)

With a workforce intelligence model, executives are able to make better informed business decisions using insights garnered from its outputs. Figure 7-2 depicts three key insights derived from Figure 7-1 and their implications and potential recommendations, or impact to business plans.

Figure 7-2

Short-Haul Class A Truck Driver			
Workforce Intelligence	**Insight**	**Implication**	**Business Planning Impact**
	1 in 4 drivers are age 55 or older	High retirement turnover risk	1. Report monthly retirement turnover metrics to General Manager and Business Unit Senior Executive 2. Offer retention bonus to "senior" drivers using a criteria of so many years of experience and a satisfactory or above performance review
12% Five-Year Supply Gap	Gen Y participation rate is lower than benchmark	High attraction risks – may not have replacement workers to backfill retirees	1. Execute a "Younger Driver" recruiting campaign 2. Offer retention bonus to retain new-hire Drivers 3. Offer bonus for anyone who refers a Gen Y Driver who is hired 4. Assess current Driver workforce culture to determine if it is aligned with an environment attractive to the workforce of the future
	Immediate industry-wide Driver demand is lower than benchmark	A slight increase in market demand could quickly trigger a workforce supply shortage	1. Offer retention bonus to high-performing Drivers 2. Create a pre-screen list of Driver candidate interested in employment and with flexible start dates 3. Offer multi-year pay to stay retention bonus for all Drivers with satisfactory or above performance review

Now, while most organizations require the insights from workforce intelligence, most do not need to develop the capabilities to build and run the models. In fact, for most organizations, it is more cost effective to purchase completed models, updated once or twice a year, from expert advisors than develop the internal capabilities.

Economic cycles will come and go over the next twenty years. While they will have a short-term affect on demand, none will alter the demographic trend shaping the working age population. We are approaching a period in time when demand for labor will out-pace supply. While this may take half a generation to come to fruition, the near-term impact is some positions will show these signs earlier than others. Whether or not your organization is hiring, this is a concern for all executives because of the realities of turnover – eventually, someone will leave your organization. Executives require workforce intelligence to determine which jobs have supply risks so mitigation plans can be designed and implemented. In the event turnover occurs in a critical position, executives using workforce intelligence capabilities will be better prepared to minimize the disruption to business operations caused from a vacancy in a critical position.

CHAPTER 8

Strengthening Success and Returns with HR Operating Improvements

Four years ago our family decided to *invest* in two dogs. Notice my verb choice. I thought all I needed to enjoy two dogs was, well, some free time and two dogs. Unfortunately, I was wrong. Many enabling objects are required to ensure enjoyment of two dogs. Take for example the invisible fence. You want the dogs to be safe when they are outside, right? Well, you need a fence to keep them from roaming into danger. Oh, not just any fence, but an electronic "invisible" fence. Then you need dog coats to keep the little guys warm during cool evening walks. Never mind that dogs have lived successfully without coats in climates more temperate than Ohio, our boys need something to keep their little bodies warm. Then there's the dog bed. I did not realize dogs snoozing on a floor were inappropriate, but I guess it is.

So, as you can see, the decision to purchase two dogs, might seem like a single, easy transaction to some. To others, though, several supporting transactions are required to accompany the procurement of two dogs.

Life has a way of doing this and while this example is personal, supporting actions are often required to reinforce the originally planned undertaking.

Some organizations are finding that the return on investment from their workforce strategy is artificially low because their current-state human resources infrastructure is insufficiently supporting this "leading-practice" initiative. If the inadequate infrastructure is not addressed, sub-par results continue which can then be followed by organizational challenges to the effectiveness and value of a workforce strategy.

Executives intent on avoiding artificially low returns on their workforce strategy are recommended to:

INSIGHT #6

*Correct Human Resources infrastructure
challenges to improve effectiveness and
returns of a Workforce Strategy*

The HR Operating Model

While HR executives are frequently aware of many of their infrastructure challenges, we still recommend a rapid diagnostics scan for thoroughness, sake. The most effective approach which we have found for this is a current state scan of the HR Operating Model, depicted in Figure 8-1.

Figure 8-1

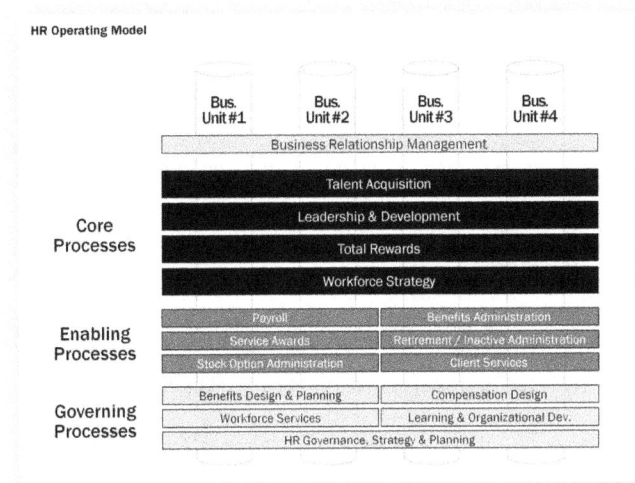

HR Operating Model

The assessment, performed in parallel to the Workforce Strategy, identifies technology, process, policy, procedure and organization opportunities that facilitate a more successful Workforce Strategy outcome.

The assessment examines three major processes of the Human Resources Operating Model: core, enabling and governing. Each major process area is examined relative to the following questions:

- Where does the performance of this process limit the Workforce Strategy's success?

- Where does this process require the most significant change to implement the Workforce Strategy?

- What are the most important Human Resources Operating Model interfaces to other business process that might be limiting the Workforce Strategy's success?

Here is a list of some of the more frequent recommendations from this type of assessment:

- *Adding staff or reallocating responsibilities within the current staff to ensure* additional activities of a workforce strategy are not jeopardized by band-width constraints

- *Updating compensation packages* to market standard to better attract critical position candidates in a tight labor market

- *Realigning the organization's culture* to incorporate the values and beliefs of the emerging generation of workers

- *Improving the speed and effectiveness of the recruiting process* to compete more effectively in a tight labor market for critical position workers

- *Upgrading HRIS technologies*

- *Producing and marketing the organization's employment brand*

- *Redesigning the human resources business relationship management role*

Improvements, like these, will facilitate a more success, not only for the workforce strategy, but for HR operations, as well. Not every organization is fortunate to have a robust HR operating model. Often, HR is underfunded, understaffed and underappreciated. A workforce strategy is an opportunity to make investments in HR that not only reinvigorates the group but also gives it enhanced capabilities for implementing a strategic business initiative.

CHAPTER 9

Aligning the Strategy's Capabilities with the Organization's Willingness to Change

Throughout this book, we have discovered much of the WHY and HOW of a workforce strategy. By that, we mean much of the book's content has focused on the justification for a workforce strategy and the insights that contribute to a breakthrough plan. However, this chapter and the next will begin our transition from the classroom to the workroom.

A maturity model is a tool for representing the progression

or development of something, like an organization, business process or technology system. Some business executives rush to a maturity model to determine how well their organization is performing, as if the tool is something like an elementary school progress report card. So, while "good," "better" and "best" interpretations are natural outcomes from most maturity models, a model's real value is its ability to help executives determine which level is "optimal" for their organization and what they need to do to grow within the level instead of maturing to the next. Here is what we mean.

In the past, more was always better. Things like "more taste", "more leg-room" or "more features" were often preferred over their lesser counterparts. Yet, within the last few years, "how much is enough" has entered our vocabulary and its ability to generate decisions about what an organization requires versus wants makes it a meaningful part of every executive's agenda.

See, the idea that "more is not always better" is rooted in the fact that with "more" comes "more costs," "more complexity," "more organizational disruption" and "more expectations." Yes, "more" also has additional features and functions, but they come at a price. This cost – benefit tradeoff — triggers many executives to choose their "optimal" location on the maturity mode instead of pursuing higher and higher levels of progression and development.

So, once an executive determines his organization's optimal level, the maturity model can then be used as a benchmark, where the executive compares his organization to the model's ideal state at a level to determine what, if any, capability gaps might exist. This feature of a maturity model is very relevant since it is possible, if not probable, that most organizations have only developed a portion of a stage's capabilities.

Organizations intent on using a Workforce Strategy Maturity Model are encouraged to:

INSIGHT #7

Use the business organization's "willingness to change" maturity level as the gauge to determine the capabilities required of the Workforce Strategy

---

There are different methods we could have used to benchmark or describe a business organization's maturity within a workforce strategy context. Some might think we should base the model on the business' understanding of or expertise in workforce issues and risks. We think this approach is, well, wrong. First, it is very subjective and second, it is very argumentative. No one wants to look "less mature" than another.

Instead, our approach is to benchmark a business organization's maturity based on its risk level, determined by its willing to change. We believe that the level of change acceptable to business predetermines the workforce problem and the portfolio of solution choices. A business organization only willing to incur small amounts of change will view the workforce challenge differently than an organization that is open to transformational change. Figure 9-1 depicts the Workforce Strategy Maturity Model.

Figure 9-1

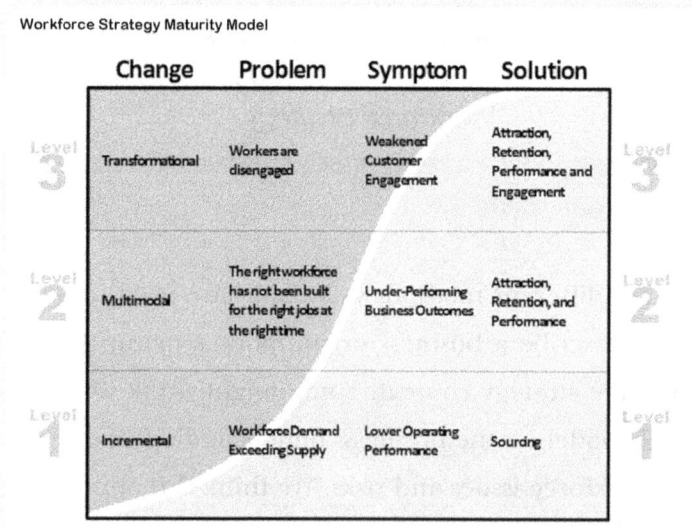

Workforce Strategy Maturity Model

	Change	Problem	Symptom	Solution
Level 3	Transformational	Workers are disengaged	Weakened Customer Engagement	Attraction, Retention, Performance and Engagement
Level 2	Multimodal	The right workforce has not been built for the right jobs at the right time	Under-Performing Business Outcomes	Attraction, Retention, and Performance
Level 1	Incremental	Workforce Demand Exceeding Supply	Lower Operating Performance	Sourcing

Level One

At Level One, nearly all business organizations view a workforce strategy as an HR project and are not really mentally prepared for HR to lead a disruptive change program. As a result, most business organizations are only comfortable with small, incremental change. This preference dictates that the workforce strategy addresses a supply gap problem caused by a demand for workers exceeding supply. Weakening operating results are observable symptoms of this problem and are frequently caused by situations where critical positions are unstaffed or employ under-qualified workers. More often than not, this situation causes organization's to explore different sourcing solutions – how HR identifies and uncovers its candidates. For a workforce strategy organization to succeed at Level One, it must develop capabilities for:

- Building a persuasive Case for Action using internal and *external* workforce data

- Understanding the demographic segments of its workforce

- Prioritizing critical positions based on mission criticality and business impact

Level Two

Level Two is where many executives and managers within the business organization accept the workforce strategy as a truly strategic business initiative. Business has been convinced of the need to have the right workforce in the right jobs at the right time and view the workforce strategy as a means to accomplishing this.

With an expanded workforce strategy viewpoint, the business organization is more likely to be open to greater levels of change. We refer to change as multimodal because often, multiple recommendations and ensuing projects are required to solve attraction, retention and performance problems in a critical position workforce. To perform at Level Two, workforce strategy organizations must be good at:

- Managing multiple, on-going projects

- Conducting incumbent analytics to uncover opportunities outside of demographic trends and talent management metrics

- Identifying HR process opportunities to enable a workforce strategy

Level Three

At Level Three the business organization is entirely on-board with a workforce strategy. By now, early critical position strategies have produced revenue growth or cost containment results that have converted any remaining skeptics. Because business now understands how crucial a high-performing critical position workforce is to a business enterprise strategy, leaders are open to all types of change, if the change has the appropriate pay-off levels. The openness for transformational change opportunities creates a possibility for the organization to explore how a workforce strategy can be used to solve a weakening customer experience brought on by a disengaged critical position workforce.

To succeed at Level Three, workforce strategy organizations must have strong expertise in:

- Framing and positioning executive level workforce issues and risks

- Collaborating with business organizations like sales, marketing, customer service and operations

- Designing persuasive workforce strategies that trigger immediate implementation activities

Maturity models are more than a theoretical tool. In the right hands, a model can help a workforce strategy executive to be more successful by:

- Aligning its solution with what the business is willing and able to implement

- Deciding which maturity level to target

- Identifying workforce strategy capability gaps

CHAPTER 10

A Guided Tour of Three Workforce Challenges

This book was written to provide executives with a toolset for strategically solving workforce challenges. A resource they can reference for ideas while building a workforce strategy. We never intended the book to be a theoretical-only discussion, so in keeping with our belief, let us explore three practical, real-life challenges and how the tools and insights from this book can be applied.

Challenge #1: Which locations have qualified labor to support organic growth?

If growth is not part of your agenda now, someday, soon, it

will be. Historical conversations about growth have focused mostly on *how* an organization will achieve its goal, as well as its strategy and tactics. Too often, the conversation does not focus on *what* the organization must coordinate — things like its human capital — to reach the goal. This is likely to change in the coming years.

As we saw in chapter one, labor market patterns are causing some executives intent on growing the business to begin questioning whether the organization has the human capital to facilitate its growth plans.

Many executives in organizations we consult with have a growing challenge of having no or limited visibility into which of their locations has the greatest abundance of labor to support an organic growth strategy. Failure to understand the workforce supply may result in some organizations over-investing in some locations and under-investing in others. This generally results in financial performance below expectations.

Addressing this challenge can be done in three steps:

Step 1. Refocus Challenge to Critical Positions

The first step is to reframe the challenge for the organization. While many jobs need to be staffed at a location, critical positions will likely be the jobs most difficult to fill. To help the organization shift its attention to and select its critical positions, try asking it to reflect on these questions:

- Which jobs are mission critical? If we do not have this job staffed we are violating a law, regulation, standard or agreement

- Which jobs have the greatest contribution to business objectives

- Which jobs are routinely poached by competitors

The result of Step 1 must be a list of critical positions for each location.

Step 2. Generate Workforce Intelligence Scans

The second step is to determine the location's supply and demand for each critical position. The only difference now, compared to the framework and approach we described in Chapter Seven, is that instead of analyzing critical position data for the entire U.S. workforce, here, we are scoping the effort to a single city. Figure 10-1 depicts a Database Engineer Workforce Intelligence Scan for Atlanta, GA.

Figure 10-1

Current Year Plus 5 Supply Gap Model – Database Engineer: Atlanta Critical Position

	Current Year	Year +1	Year +2	Year +3	Year +4	Year +5
DEMAND						
Sector Demand	3,150	3,276	3,407	3,543	3,685	3,832
TOTAL DEMAND	3,150	3,276	3,407	3,543	3,685	3,832
SUPPLY						
Employed	3,139	3,265	3,396	3,532	3,600	3,671
Unemployed	183	190	179	186	170	173
Other Qualfied Workers	129	134	139	145	148	151
Retirees Re-Entering Workforce	15	16	17	18	27	28
Retirees Leaving Workforce	(298)	(310)	(340)	(353)	(540)	(551)
TOTAL SUPPLY	3,167	3,294	3,391	3,527	3,405	3,471
Supply Gap	17	18	(16)	(16)	(280)	(361)
Supply Gap Percentage	1%	1%	(0%)	(0%)	(8%)	(10%)

When analyzing the data, seek to determine:

1. *Critical Mass:* Independent of whether or not there are available workers is an assessment of the overall number of workers in the location. Does this location have a sufficient number of workers to fuel my growth, regardless of availability? You will find that many locations only have depth in some critical position workforces, but not all.

2. *Available Supply:* This is the more traditional supply/ demand gap assessment we have discussed throughout this book. Knowing how hard you may need to

work to recruit and retain critical position workers is a key-decision criterion that needs to be factored into growth plans.

Figure 10-2 shows how you could present the analysis for Available Supply. The chart depicts the critical positions, organized in rows, and the locations, listed in columns. Harvey Balls are used to depict a relative assessment of available supply. For most audiences, relative assessments of supply are more than sufficient to communicate findings. We recommend, in most presentations, not depicting specific numerical data since it seems to have a tendency to invite very specific, sometimes non-relevant questions.

Figure 10-2

Available Supply

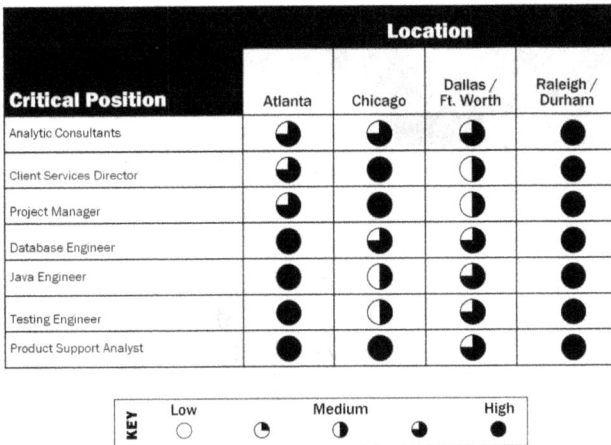

Critical Position	Location			
	Atlanta	Chicago	Dallas / Ft. Worth	Raleigh / Durham
Analytic Consultants	◕	◕	◕	●
Client Services Director	◕	●	◔	●
Project Manager	◕	●	◔	●
Database Engineer	●	◕	◕	●
Java Engineer	●	◑	◕	●
Testing Engineer	●	◑	◕	●
Product Support Analyst	●	●	◕	●

KEY: Low ○ ◔ Medium ◑ ◕ High ●

Step 3. Incorporate Business Criteria into Decision Model

The third step is to evaluate the locations relative to other business-impacting workforce criteria [Figure 10-3] such as:

- Ten-year projected population and workforce growth rate

- Business Cost Index

- Labor Cost Index

- Quality of Living Index

- Percent of Critical Position Workforce Ages 18-29

Figure 10-3

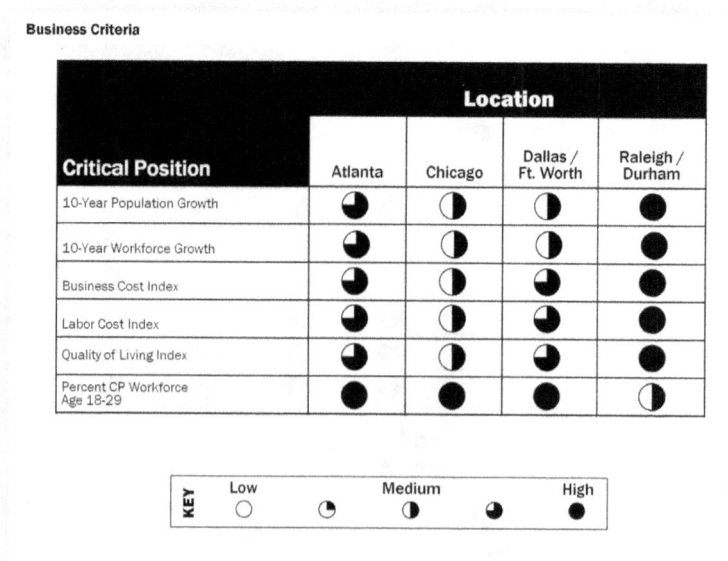

The analysis contained in Steps 2 and 3 are sufficient for most executives to begin making a more informed business decision regarding which locations hold the best possible labor market conditions to support an organic growth strategy.

Challenge #2: What is our retirement risk exposure?

Because of the aging population phenomenon, the first thing our consulting client CEOs want to know is the organization's retirement risk exposure. With retirements, an organization can be quickly depleted of its knowledge and expertise. For organizations relying on a highly skilled workforce, retirements are a real threat to its competitiveness.

Organizations can begin to assess its retirement challenge in two steps:

Step 1. Determine Retirement Eligible Workforce for the Organization

Most executives are curious to know what percentage of the total workforce is eligible to retire in five years. Other than solving a curiosity and maybe benchmarking the organization, the initial figure does not influence retirement intervention what so ever. This is because retirement interventions are focused on a critical position, while this step focuses on the organization.

With that in mind, to calculate the retirement percentage, you first need to identify the retirement eligibility rules. In many organizations this requires determining rules for not only defined benefits, but also defined contribution plans.

Take a data extract of the HRIS and run two queries against the current workforce for these rules. For example, at one organization, we began with the defined benefits program. This organization's plan has two rules to determine retirement eligibility: *55 years of age with 30 years of service* OR *62 years of age with 18 years of service.* When we ran a query against the current workforce data set, we determined there are 622 workers in the next five years who are eligible for retirement under the defined benefits program. This means that 622 current workers met one of our two rules under this plan. Next, we focused on the defined contribution plan which had a single retirement eligible rule: *55 years of age and five years of service.* The query found that the organization has 1,659 who meet the single defined contribution. Together, 2,281 workers are eligible to retire in the next five years.

Next, we take the 2,281 eligible workers and convert it to a percentage of the total workforce, which at the time was 10,373 workers. The result is 22% (2,281/10,373=22%). Now, 22% is just a number. At this point, we cannot tell if it is a "good" number or a "bad" number. We need to have something to compare it with. The figure we use to add context to the retirement percentage is 15%. Any organization whose five-year retirement eligibility percentage is greater than or equal to 15% is considered to be over-exposed to retirement risks. Figure 10-4 shows the build-up of retirement eligible workers over the five-year period.

Figure 10-4

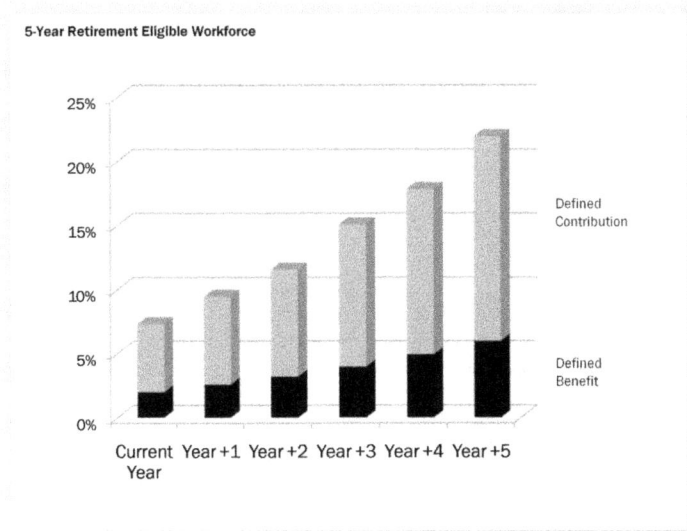

5-Year Retirement Eligible Workforce

Now, here is the confusing part for some. While the organization, at a whole, is at risk when it is at or above 15%, mitigating interventions are not designed at the organization level. They are only designed and implemented at the critical position level. Therefore, the workforce strategist, should proceed to Step 2 and begin identifying which critical positions are driving this figure.

Step 2. Determine Retirement Eligible Workforce for Critical Positions

Step 2 is very similar to Step 1, except the calculations now group workers by critical position. It is not necessary to perform the retirement eligible calculation for every position in the organization. The output of this step is a list of critical positions whose retirement eligible workforce is greater than or equal to 15%. These positions are those which need immediate interventions. Figure 10-5 depicts an example output from Step 2.

Figure 10-5

5-Year Retirement Eligible Critical Position Analysis

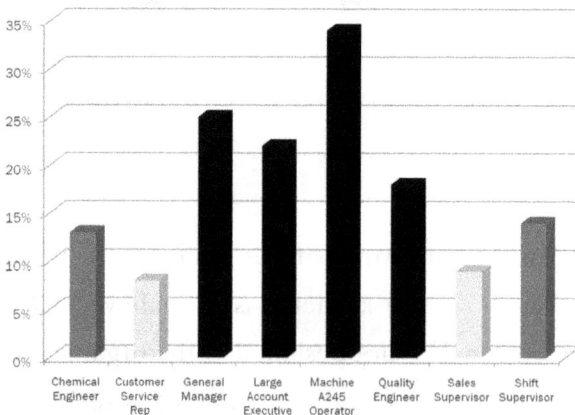

Challenge #3: Do we have a projected 5-year internal critical position supply gap?

Chapter 1 demonstrated that 46% of the U.S. occupations are at or near full employment at any given time. This is the result of a three-and-a-half year study into workforce supply. Given the magnitude of occupations at or near full employment, there are many organizations that will experience a shortage of qualified workers for their critical positions in the next three years.

The problem is, many of these critical position shortages go undetected. Here is what we mean. To compensate for not having qualified candidates for a position, organizations sometimes lower the skill requirements to identify more prospective workers. If this leads to accepted offers, over time, a gap may begin to emerge between the skill requirements of the critical position and the capabilities of the workforce.

We frequently see this with technical sales positions. Most technical sales jobs require a technical undergraduate degree, either in computer science or engineering, frequently an M.B.A, and three to five years of experience with a specific sector, product or service. Those who have made this journey and are qualified are few are far between. In fact, for years, demand has out-paced supply for qualified workers.

To enable an aggressive revenue goal, an organization requires so many sales executives per millions of dollars in revenue. Each organization has its benchmark figure. Now, no one wants to tell the CEO that the annual revenue plan is in jeopardy because the organization cannot find qualified sales executives, so what begins to happen is the hiring requirements are relaxed, allowing staffing goals to be achieved. *Somewhere in the organization, an executive has just checked-off Milestone #1 from his list of annual plan activities.*

Unfortunately, while the CEO is relaxed, thinking he has the sales organization to fuel growth, the reality is the new employees are under-qualified. So, where as a new, qualified, technical sales executive can generate $2 million dollars in revenue in the first year, a lesser qualified worker, may only be able to generate $750,000 to $1 million in revenue. The net result is that while the CEO and others believe they have the *right workers in the right jobs at the right time*, the truth is, they have, in some cases, the "wrong" workers in the right jobs and the difference in qualifications is going to result in a missed revenue plan.

When a sales organization has too many under-qualified workers, the ensuing result is something like what we have depicted in Figure 10-6.

Figure 10-6

Worsening Workforce Situation Example

Sales Quotas Missed

Revenue Growth Slows

Tension Builds Between
Executives and Sales Force

Sales Force Engagement Falls

Revenue Growth Slows, Further

Sales Force Voluntary and
Involuntary Turnover Increases

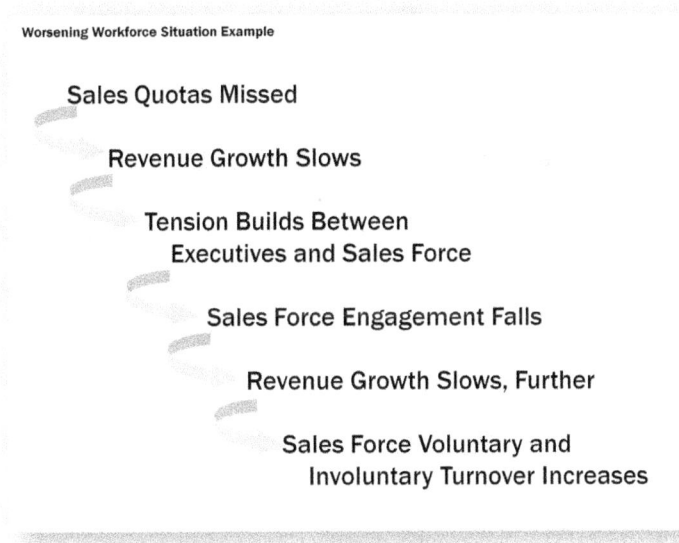

Now, too often, the failed revenue goals are blamed on a portion of the sales workforce who did not meet revenue goals. The issue we have here, though, is not a performance problem, as many executives believe. The original workforce problem is a shortage issue, not performance. While in some instances lesser-qualified workers could be hired, performance goals must be adjusted. This may result in additional workers being required to achieve the goal and higher labor expenses. Either course of action has a cost. The question is, which cost do you want to incur? Whatever you do, though, call a zebra a zebra. Do not blame missed targets on performance issues when less-qualified workers have been hired to compensate for supply challenges.

In our workshops, we show, in detail, how to build a model to assess supply gaps. Here is a synopsis of those steps:

Step 1. Estimate Annual Demand for the Critical Position

While most organizations are clear on their current year staffing plan, visibility into staffing projections in a three-to-five-year period becomes very fuzzy. Here's where you can begin, if you need a place to start.

Use your organization's current year revenue plan and the current staffing plan to determine the revenue per critical position worker. Next, use your organization's three-to-five-year revenue forecast, and applying the revenue per critical position worker, back into how many workers are required to support the projected revenue figure. Now, if you want to get a little fancy you can incorporate:

a)   Year on Year Productivity Improvements

Build into the model a factor for productivity improvements from year to year. For example, if in Year 1 you need 11 engineers to support $10 million in revenue, in Year 2, you may only need 10 engineers to support the same $10 million because the engineers are now more skilled at their job.

b)   Year to Year Flow Variables

Build into the model what we call "flow" variables that account for staff reductions from year to year. Consider planning for:

• Promotions or lateral movements out of a critical position

• Voluntary and Involuntary turnover

• Retirements

The point is, if you have 100 engineers at the start of Year 1, by Year 2, you will not have the same 100 engineers, assuming zero hires. Some will leave the company; some may be promoted, etc. The result is, you actually start the year off with maybe 85 engineers out of that 100.

Now, not all critical positions can be estimated from revenue, so this is not a blanket solution. For example, in many situations, you need a client manager per account. Some accounts may be smaller, say $1million in revenue, while others may be larger, say $30 million in revenue, but each account still has one full-time client manager. Here, the staffing driver is not revenues, but the number of accounts.

Regardless of the estimating approach, Step 1 needs to generate a three-to-five-year demand for the critical position.

Step 2. Estimate the Supply for the Critical Position

The Supply estimate for a critical position is made up of a number of components. The components for an internal Workforce Intelligence Scan are similar to those in Chapter 7 of an external scan. Remember, not all apply to every Scan, so, choose the ones that are relevant and build them into your model. They are:

- *Employed* Critical Position Workers– The qualified workers employed in the occupation.

- *Recently Laid-Off Critical Position Workers* – The qualified workers who are either required or whom you may want to recall to support future demand.

- *Other Qualified Workers* – Workers in similar jobs within the organization who could be retrained and deployed for the critical position.

- *Hires* – The number of hires you expect to be able to process. This is not necessarily the number the organization needs, but what its current talent supply chain is able to reasonably recruit, hire and bring onboard. So, do not plan for 12 new hires a month if your current organization is only able to process, at most, five or six. Doing so, will give a false output from our model.

- *Turnover* – An estimate of the number of workers leaving the position, both voluntary and involuntary.

- *Retirees Leaving the Critical Position* – An estimate of the number of workers exiting the organization's critical position workforce due to retirement.

- *Retirees Re-Entering the Workforce* – An estimate of the number of retires whom, if you organization permits, is able to rehire, either as a full or part-time employee or as a contractor. In reality, this estimate can either be your retirees or another organization's retires. The point of this line-item is to encourage the organization to think about hiring not-traditional workers. This estimate may be hard to make and might be zero for many organizations.

- *Mid-Career Workers Reentering the Workforce* – An estimate of the number of workers who are reentering the workforce after being out of the labor market for a number of years. For example, some females leave the workforce when they begin raising a family. Once the children become school age, they often return to the workforce. Again, the point of this line-item is to encourage the organization to think about hiring non-traditional workers. This estimate may be hard to make and might be zero for many organizations.

The result of Step 2 is a supply estimate, developed from HRIS data and internal assumptions.

Step 3. Net the Demand and Supply Estimates to Determine Any Gap

Figure 10-7

Current Year Plus 5 Supply Gap Model – Technical Sales Executive Critical Position

	Current Year	Year +1	Year +2	Year +3	Year +4	Year +5
DEMAND						
Sales Executive Demand	117	128	143	164	194	236
TOTAL DEMAND	117	128	143	164	194	236
SUPPLY						
Current Sales Executives	108	117	127	137	147	154
Other Qualified Sales Executives	3	4	4	5	7	8
Hires	12	14	18	20	20	20
Turnover	(8)	(8)	(15)	(19)	(23)	(26)
Retirees Leaving	0	0	0	0	0	0
Retirees Reentering	1	1	2	2	2	2
Mid-Career Reentering	0	0	1	1	1	2
TOTAL SUPPLY	117	127	137	147	154	160
Supply Gap	0	0	(6)	(18)	(40)	(76)
Supply Gap Percentage	0%	0%	(4%)	(12%)	(26%)	(47%)

When Step 1 and 2 estimates are combined, you have something that looks like Figure 10-7, depending on how many years are included in the forecast and the specific supply components used in the model.

Once the model is developed, begin analyzing it for findings and conclusions which can be used to make better, more informed management decisions. Using our example, here is what this Workforce Intelligence Scan says to us: Within two years, the organization will begin to experience a supply gap. This gap is the result of three factors

- *Aggressive growth targets.* These sales executives are required to drive the revenue projections of the strategic plan

- *Current constraints in our ability to attract hires.* This is due to an unknown employment brand in the marketplace and internal process constraints on our ability to recruit, hire and onboard candidates. The result is a projected maximum of 20 hires a year, under the current system. Before it is assumed that only branding and process improvements will resolve this issue, an external labor market study should be conducted. This will help us determine if technical sales executives exist in the quantity our projections require.

- *Emerging turnover issues.* Past experiences with rapid growth have shown that these periods also bring an above average turnover. The estimates include both voluntary and involuntary departures.

So, an exercise like this gives executives insights into future attraction and retention challenges with time to make course corrections. While whatever is entered into the model will be wrong — situations change very quickly — the model serves as a reference point for identifying challenges before they strike.

CLOSING THOUGHTS

Shortly after the Great Chicago Fire of 1871, a group of businessmen examined the city's remains and met to discuss the future; one dominant and dismal view point emerged. Understandable, given that everyone in the group had their business destroyed by the fire. After much debate, all, except one, decided to leave Chicago and start over in a more promising region of the country. The businessman who chose to stay and rebuild was Marshall Fields, one of the most successful merchants in history. After the fire, what he saw was opportunity!

Both interpretations were correct. It is not as though there was a wrong answer, yet, how each interpreted his situation after the fire shaped the following years of his life.

The same can be said about our workforce. I agree that at this time, the U.S. does have a considerable number of unemployed workers. Yet, I also believe that those who hold this as their dominant point of view will be severely challenged to put the *right workers* in the *right jobs* at the *right time.*

The point of view which I sincerely hope you share with me is that while we have an abundance of labor, sectors of our economy have a shortage of skilled and qualified workers for certain critical positions. I firmly believe that those who hold this alternative thought and transmit it into effective action using the concepts explained in this book will be rewarded by the market.

I wish you much success!

Repurposing the Breakthrough Workforce Strategy

This epilogue represents a close collaboration be-tween R.B. Stroud (Bob) and Eric. While all the concepts were co-developed, sections of the epilogue were frequently written by one person. We thought it might be beneficial for readers to have an awareness of the section authors, so, sections written by Bob are preceded by his initials, RBS, and Eric by EJS.

E J S

Introduction

The opportunity to apply ***Breakthrough Workforce Strategy*** to solve a similar, but different workforce challenge evolved out of many conversations with R.B. (Bob) Stroud. Bob is a talent management executive advisor with expertise in moving workforces through paradigm shifts. While Bob collaborates with leaders on key talent management decisions, his art is engaging workers of all convictions to craft a new work environment for their organization. In addition to his management consulting position, Bob contributes his employee-focused expertise in other roles, including board member for a regional workforce investment board and advisor and speaker to non-profit organizations serving displaced workers.

Soon after discovering our Public Sector *Breakthrough*, I asked Bob if he would co-author a closing chapter for the book. To my delight, he agreed. Bob's expertise and insights were instrumental in building-out the solution contained here. I am grateful Bob agreed to write this chapter with me. I could not have accomplished it without him.

New Applications for *Breakthrough Workforce Strategy*

Breakthrough Workforce Strategy was primarily written for employers. The framework, insights templates and examples all focus on challenges of organizations that hire and retain workers. Within the last year, though, I have come to realize that the work assembled for *Breakthrough Workforce Strategy* is applicable to *Public Sector Organizations* (PSOs) or government agencies that fund and manage programs for laid-off, veteran and aging workers. Examples of these organizations at the federal level are: Department of Labor – Employment & Training Administration, Senior Community Service Employment Program, National Farm Worker Jobs Program, and Key to Career Success Military Transition Program. Many states have similar organizations and are frequently called One-Stop Career Centers or Employment Services Offices.

With Bob's employee-focused experience, we discovered how *Breakthrough Workforce Strategy's* insights around critical positions apply to PSOs to produce:

o A higher velocity of displaced workers transitioning into full-time jobs

o Greater regional economic benefits

o A workforce development program more synchronized with employer demand

R B S

Why PSOs Should Consider an Alternative Model

Most PSOs have it correct. Matching the supply of workers to the market's demand for skills in many instances connects employers with staffing needs to unemployed workers in need of opportunities. Now, while matching supply with demand is sound, we believe it can and should be enhanced.

Based on the following considerations, we believe the go-forward employment market will be dramatically different from the last 25 years.

A 25-Year Economic Boom

Today's PSOs are working in a new employment environment and as a result, their charter of returning underemployed and unemployed workers to full-time and meaningful work is a daunting challenge. The U.S. economy is growing at an anemic level, somewhere between 2.0% and 2.5% of Gross Domestic Product (GDP). The impact of 2.0% - 2.5%, growth is fewer employment opportunities are being created to return laid-off, veteran and aging workers to jobs. In fact, at current growth rates, it will take *three to five* more years before the economy produces enough jobs to re-employ jobless workers and *six to eight* years if we included underemployed, marginally attached and discouraged workers. How different is this than recent history? Significantly different!

December 2007 marked the end to the longest post-war expansion in history. While the economy registered a recession in 1990 and 1991, its duration (eight months) and GDP impact (-0.3%) were minimal compared to the growth experienced from November 1982 until November 2007 (well over 300%). During the 25 year expansion, the U.S. economy grew at an annual rate of 5.9%. At one point, our economy grew in one three-year period an average of 9%! Rather different than today, isn't it?

If the U.S. economy was on fire, then it was "white-hot." Prior to this period, most living adults would have considered a normal expansion period to be between four to five years. This expansion beat all expectations.

Now, the impact of this expansion was significant to PSOs serving displaced workers. *The strong economy pulled many unemployed into the workforce.* Because of the robust economy, enhancements to the supply-demand approach were not relevant. Other challenges needed attention, like finding workers for the new jobs being created.

Now, while the economic climate is much different today than it was over the past 20 to 25 years, there are three other macro factors which we believe are shaping a future much different than the present and will eventually alter the landscape for PSOs.

Global Outsourcing

The concept of outsourcing started to show-up in the 1970s as U.S. organizations built-up company-owned operations in lower-cost countries. It was not until the economic pressure from the 1980s recessions did these companies refocus on their core operations and begin outsourcing jobs. What started out as the outsourcing of factory, call center and data entry jobs has evolved into higher-skilled positions like computer engineer, bio-tech researcher, tax preparer and financial analyst. In fact, by some estimates, as much as 22% to 29% of all U.S jobs possess some characteristics that would make them susceptible to outsourcing.

While no one can say for certain how many jobs have been lost to outsourcing, one outcome is true. The number of jobs performed by U.S. workers is smaller due to outsourcing. This fact has a real implication for PSOs. The jobs requiring workers and the number of workers in-demand will be different than today.

Green Economy

Green seems to be the new color. People now talk of green jobs, green construction practices and green products. Seems like a refreshing color considering many organizations in 2008 and 2009 were feverishly working to avoid the "red."

So, what is a green job? The Department of Labor - Bureau of Labor and Statistics defines it as a job:

- *In a business that produces goods or provides services that benefit the environment or conserve natural resources.*

- *In which a worker's duties involve making the establishment's production processes more environmentally friendly or use fewer natural resources.*

The green economy is going to have a large impact on our future workforce. Using the Bureau of Labor and Statistics definition, we estimate that in 2010, alone, approximately 15% of the workforce is in green jobs. That amount is equal to the total combined workforces of New York City, Los Angeles, Chicago, Dallas-Ft. Worth and Washington D.C. I imagine you had no idea the green economy workforce was that large?

The emergence of green occupations has three implications for PSOs

1. Additional workers will be required for certain jobs because the green economy will increase demand for their product or service. A great example is a business driver who will see an increase in his services as the more citizens choose public transportation to reduce pollution and conserve energy.

2. Existing workers will require retraining because the green economy will require additional skills for their job. An example of this is a construction project manager who will need to be knowledgeable of green materials and construction procedures.

3. Additional workers with new and different skills will be

required for opportunities in the green economy. An example of this is a solar engineer who is knowledgeable of current and emerging solar technologies.

The implication for PSOs is that the jobs requiring workers, the number of workers in-demand and the skills required to be proficient in those jobs will continue to change.

Technology Development

For decades we have heard about how technology is reshaping worker skills, but, often, we have no idea what that really means. Twenty years ago, when someone was referred to as a technology-skilled worker, depending on the career field, it often meant they knew a half-dozen DOS commands, could create a Microsoft PowerPoint presentation or import data from a database into an Excel spreadsheet. While this may mirror a 1995-era technology-skilled worker, it is not even close to depicting the same worker, today or even 25 years from now.

So, what does it mean to be a technology-skilled worker? For the general, non-information technology worker, it means being knowledgeable of the tools, procedures, language, and materials of an occupation. Really, it is that simple. Do not be confused by the word technology. No longer does it mean "desktop" computers. Instead, if you are an airplane mechanic, it means knowing how to use computerized shop equipment and having an awareness of the electronic components of airplanes. See, today, an airplane mechanic very rarely reaches for the airline mechanic kit containing wrenches, pliers, screwdrivers and sheet metal equipment to diagnose a problem. Rather, the mechanic connects and uses a computerized diagnostics machine to determine if components and systems of the airplane are secure and working properly.

The implication for PSOs is that the skills required to be proficient in future jobs will continue to evolve.

So, together, a slower and greener economy and global outsourcing and technology development are combining to alter the landscape for PSOs. How they serve displaced workers needs to change. That does not mean if they continue as they have, they will fail. No, rather, what we mean is we believe there is a "new approach" that could possibly be more helpful in shaping their "new landscape."

E J S

Why a Critical Position Approach

A core theme for **Breakthrough Workforce Strategy** is critical positions. Through several conversations, Bob and I started to wonder if the concept of jobs that are either *mission critical* or *highly business impacting* AND *hard to staff* could apply to

PSOs that retrain displaced workers. We believe that PSOs can use critical positions to enhance their approach to matching supply with demand.

Matching supply with demand seems like a rather simple concept until you are asked to implement it. The supply side of the concept is predetermined, given the focus of the PSO, namely laid-off, veteran and aging workers. With supply known, it seems to us the nagging question really is: "What is meant by demand?"

If you have ever been asked to pick-up a bottle of barbecue sauce at the market, then you have an idea of the complexity associated with answering our question. Wandering down the grocery aisle displaying barbecue sauces can be overwhelming. Before we can even begin narrowing the plethora of choices, we first need to decide if we were asked for a barbecue sauce or possibly a barbecue marinade. Then, depending on how we resolve that question, we might need to decide on a sub-category including, marinade-only, a product that doubles as a marinade and basting sauce or just a one-dimensional barbecue sauce. Now, if we stay within the one-dimensional sauce family of products, we might need to decide if we need a sweet, mustard-based or vinegar-based sauce. Then we might need to decide if we need a hot sauce or a mild sauce. Whew...

See, something as easy-sounding as picking-up a bottle of

barbecue sauce is much more complicated than it might appear to some. In fact, it is very similar to the question we presented in Chapter Three *"which workforce is the focus of a workforce strategy."* This question was equally challenging to answer at first.

Now, when most PSO's refer to demand, they mean it as the skills required for today's employment vacancies plus tomorrow's emerging workforce opportunities. Fundamentally, this viewpoint is correct. Our single recommendation is to enhance it using the critical position concept explained in Chapter Three.

How a Critical Position Approach Can Be Applied to PSO's

Applying a critical position approach suggests that PSO's identify market-demanded skills based on either the job's mission criticality or its business impact and hard to fill assessment. Instead of training programs aligned with the current view of demand, a critical position strategy aligns training with the skills required for today's critical position employment vacancies plus tomorrow's emerging critical position workforce opportunities.

To some, this may seem like a small "tweak" – maybe even "word smithing," but our workforce strategy model is designed around a strategic concept of *small change – large effect.* Chapter Three listed the characteristics of critical positions. We have selected from this list those relevant to PSOs and added to it their implication. Together, they form a strong argument for why PSO's should adopt a critical position approach for their demand model [Figure 11-1].

Figure 11-1

CRITICAL POSITION CHARACTERISTICS & IMPLICATIONS FOR PSO	
CRITICAL POSITION CHARACTERISTIC INSIGHT	IMPLICATION TO PSO
Critical position unemployment rates are almost always lower than the national average.	PSO's will see a faster time to employment and higher employment rates for graduates of critical position training programs. Combined, this means a higher return of training dollars invested.
Staffing a critical position takes at least twice as long as the average position.	Employers are challenged to source and recruit critical position workers and would value a PSO creating a pool of trained workers.
Critical position supply lags demand during growth periods.	PSOs can be assured that there is a real and immediate need for critical position skills if current vacancies exist.
When supply lags demand, demand is strongest for critical positions requiring extensive experience and capabilities.	Supports the need for PSOs to provide skill-specific training that might not be available otherwise

What does a critical position approach mean to a PSO? It means a PSO begins assessing current job vacancies for those that are critical positions and aligning training programs with these skill requirements. A critical position approach does not mean that the PSO is no longer training and staffing for other jobs. In fact, the majority of the training and development efforts can continue, as planned. This approach is not necessarily an *Either-OR* approach. Instead, it is something occurs in parallel or in addition to current training and staffing efforts. What a PSO does less of is treating every job as though it is equal.

R | B | S

What is Required of PSOs

PSOs adopting this approach will require certain key capabilities, among them to:

1. Select and prioritize critical positions from job inventory

The first challenge will be to determine the specific criteria PSOs will use to determine what makes a job a critical position. For example, it is not enough to say that a job has to be business impacting. PSOs will need to define business impacting in terms of a specific, measureable and time-bound metrics. Once the criteria are defined, it can be applied against the current inventory jobs which they are helping employers source to identify which are critical positions.

2. Identify tomorrow's emerging critical position workforce opportunities

It is important for PSOs to collaborate with their employer partners to forecast demand for critical position. With an understanding of the regional economy's critical positions, now and say, in the next three years, and their likely demand forecast, PSOs can better position themselves to shape and supply the workforce of the future and stimulate economic growth.

3. Redirect resources to programs focused on critical position skill development

After the critical positions have been identified from the current inventory of jobs (Point No. 1), PSOs will need to allocate resources to ensure they have the programs and capacity to redeploy workers into these jobs.

Summary

PSOs have a significant challenge. The devastating Great Recession rendered many unemployed and the slow-growing economy cannot seem to create new jobs fast enough. Add to this environment a labor market that is being transformed by outsourcing, the green economy and technology development and we will witness a changing workforce landscape where the jobs requiring workers, the number of workers in-demand and the skills required to be proficient in those jobs evolve.

It is not that PSOs are doing something wrong. Matching supply with demand is the right approach, if one exists. What we are offering is an enhancement to this approach, a parallel program where positions that are "critical" to the regional economy, now and in the future, are identified. PSOs and regional employers can then collaborate on developing a supply of workers to satisfy demand and generate economic growth.

INDEX OF SUBJECTS

www.ingramcontent.com/pod-product-compliance
Lightning Source LLC
Chambersburg PA
CBHW070406200326
41518CB00011B/2082